Your K-5 Literacy Instruction Questions Answered

HEIDI ANNE MESMER, Ph.D., and KATIE HILDEN, Ph.D.

Publishing Credits

Corinne Burton, M.A.Ed., *President* and *Publisher*
Aubrie Nielsen, M.S.Ed., *EVP of Content Development*
Kyra Ostendorf, M.Ed., *Publisher, professional books*
Véronique Bos, *Vice President of Creative*
Cathy Hernandez, *Senior Content Manager*
Courtenay Fletcher, *Cover Designer*
Colleen Pidel, *Interior Designer*
Patricia Corpuz, *Graphic Designer*

Image Credits:

All images from Shutterstock

Library of Congress Cataloging-in-Publication Data

Names: Mesmer, Heidi Anne E., author. | Hilden, Katie, author.
Title: There's research for that : your K-5 literacy instruction questions answered / Heidi Anne Mesmer and Katie Hilden
Description: Huntington Beach, CA : Shell Educational Publishing, Inc., 2025. | Includes bibliographical references and index. | Summary: "In this book, the authors present 20 common questions classroom teachers ask about teaching reading, unpack what the research actually says in answer those questions, and offer examples of how to apply that research to instruction. This book fills a gap in professional books related to the science of reading research. Too often, classroom teachers are trying desperately to stay on stop of the Science of Reading, but their efforts to find answers lead to imprecise and often misleading ideas and practices. The authors provide just the right amount of information, along with the implications for teaching"-- Provided by publisher.
Identifiers: LCCN 2024033357 (print) | LCCN 2024033358 (ebook) | ISBN 9798765971734 (paperback) | ISBN 9798765971758 (ebook)
Subjects: LCSH: Reading (Elementary) | Reading--Research.
Classification: LCC LB1573 .M4516 2025 (print) | LCC LB1573 (ebook) | DDC 372.4--dc23/eng/20240913
LC record available at https://lccn.loc.gov/2024033357
LC ebook record available at https://lccn.loc.gov/2024033358

The classroom teacher may reproduce copies of materials in this book for classroom use only. The reproduction of any part for an entire school or school system is strictly prohibited. No part of this publication may be transmitted, stored, or recorded in any form without written permission from the publisher.

Website addresses included in this book are public domain and may be subject to changes or alterations of content after publication of this product. Shell Education does not take responsibility for the future accuracy or relevance and appropriateness of website addresses included in this book. Please contact the company if you come across any inappropriate or inaccurate website addresses, and they will be corrected in product reprints.

All companies, websites, and products mentioned in this book are registered trademarks of their respective owners or developers and are used in this book strictly for editorial purposes. No commercial claim to their use is made by the author or the publisher.

A division of Teacher Created Materials
5482 Argosy Avenue
Huntington Beach, CA 92649-1039
www.tcmpub.com/shell-education
ISBN 979-8-7659-7173-4

© 2025 Shell Educational Publishing, Inc.

Printed by: 70548
Printed in: China
PO#: 14517

I dedicate this book to my children,
Davison and Lindy, for their patience
with me and for all the joy and love that
they bring into my life.
—Heidi Anne Mesmer

I dedicate this book to my daughter,
a fellow bibliophile, and to
my husband for his constant
support and patience.
—Katie Hilden

Table of Contents

INTRODUCTION 1

PART 1: FOUNDATIONAL SKILLS THAT SUPPORT WORD RECOGNITION

QUESTION 1: I know that "letter of the week" is not the way to go, but how many letters should I teach per week? 17

QUESTION 2: Should I teach letter names or letter sounds? 23

QUESTION 3: What are print concepts, and should they be given instructional attention? Don't students just naturally learn print concepts as we teach them to read? 29

QUESTION 4: Which phonological awareness skills are most important to teach, and how should I teach them? 39

QUESTION 5: What does the research say about sound walls and teaching mouth moves? 49

QUESTION 6: What does the research say about how decodable texts impact readers? How should I use decodable texts? 55

QUESTION 7: How many times does a reader need to decode a word in order to really learn it? 63

QUESTION 8: How should I teach high-frequency sight words? Should students just memorize them visually? 71

QUESTION 9: Is invented spelling supported by research? Is it damaging to children's later reading and writing? 81

QUESTION 10: Kids spend so much time on phones and computers, do they really need to be taught handwriting? 89

PART 2: LANGUAGE AND OTHER SKILLS THAT SUPPORT COMPREHENSION

QUESTION 11: For oral reading practice, should students read the same text repeatedly or read different texts? 99

QUESTION 12: What types of texts should we use when working on reading with expression? 105

QUESTION 13: What are key components of effective instructional routines for vocabulary? 113

QUESTION 14: Should I teach comprehension strategies one at a time by week? 123

QUESTION 15: Which comprehension strategies are most important to teach, and how many should I teach? Are there certain groups or combinations of strategies that work best? 129

QUESTION 16: How can I effectively teach expository text structures, and when should this instruction start? 135

QUESTION 17: Is explicit instruction of sentence comprehension necessary, and if so, what should it look like? 145

QUESTION 18: How do executive skills and cognitive flexibility impact students' reading comprehension, and how can I improve those skills? 153

QUESTION 19: How do I support my students' developing oral language? 161

QUESTION 20: Should I match students to books by reading level? If so, how? 169

REFERENCES 177
INDEX 195
ACKNOWLEDGMENTS 201
ABOUT THE AUTHORS 202

Introduction

Why We Wrote This Book

As faculty members at universities, teacher educators, and researchers, we have been both excited and concerned by the recent focus on the Science of Reading (SoR). We are excited because we believe research is a very important tool for guiding K–12 literacy instruction. It helps to know what works and how to help students. In the past few years, we have collaborated with teachers who are working to deepen and broaden their knowledge base about reading development and improve their instruction. We have also met many elementary teachers and reading specialists who are actively reexamining and shifting their reading instruction, due to state and district mandates as well as their own research and desire to meet their students' needs. We have heard the mantra "We do better when we know better" in countless conversations.

Yet we have found the current movement a bit concerning as well. At times, the language around the Science of Reading can feel judgmental and even accusatory. Sometimes we worry that teachers interpret "research says" as "just do what we tell you." This is not only disrespectful to professional educators but it is bound to fail. It is the reason that many teachers roll their eyes at all the intensity around the Science of Reading movement and close their doors so they can go back to relying on intuition and tradition with their students. Sadly, many findings that are forwarded as SoR are flawed translations of the science. They can be dated, incomplete, and misapplied.

Another concern that we have is that sometimes the phrase *Science of Reading* feels like yet another buzzword to be slapped onto a collection of practices or products, often without any real thought as to what the science really says. SoR has the potential to become a kind of groupthink—these strategies, terms, posters, and curricula *are* SoR, and these *are not*. Then it all becomes a superficial game of saying the right things to be in the SoR "club." When teachers and administrators tell us their instruction and curriculum is based on the Science of Reading, we will often ask, "What does Science of Reading mean or include? What is it NOT?" and "What research are you reading?" Let's examine the *Science of Reading* label and discuss the role of reading research.

So, What Really Is the Science of Reading?

What is the Science of Reading? According to the Reading League (n.d.), it is defined in the following way:

> The science of reading is a vast, interdisciplinary body of scientifically based research about reading and issues related to reading and writing.
>
> This research has been conducted over the last five decades across the world, and it is derived from thousands of studies conducted in multiple languages. The science of reading has culminated in a preponderance of evidence to inform how proficient reading and writing develop; why some have difficulty; and how we can most effectively assess and teach and, therefore, improve student outcomes through prevention of and intervention for reading difficulties. (para. 1–2)

We agree with this inclusive, broad, interdisciplinary definition. In contrast, we are frustrated by narrow interpretations of the Science of Reading that limit SoR to structured phonics instruction for developing readers. Despite such narrow language surrounding the Science of Reading, we believe that research can be the classroom teacher's best friend, if shared in accurate, succinct, and useful ways. For us, a bit of an epiphany occurred when Heidi Anne, active on social media, began to try to translate SoR research findings for teachers. In simple slides with research citations, she translated research into easy-to-understand language applied directly to the classroom and got overwhelmingly positive results! Teachers retweeted, commented, and dug into studies. They were hungry for findings and wanted to apply the best research in their classrooms. Quite simply, we became inspired by the questions that teachers were asking about reading research. Together, as we began to read more research studies, research reviews, or meta-analyses, we discovered a treasure trove of information that delighted, amazed, and sometimes puzzled us. We found that some of our own long-held beliefs were shattered and replaced with newfound insights from new studies or close rereadings of existing research studies.

What Is Research?

So, what is research? Quite literally, it means "to search again." There is something that the researcher doesn't know, or wants to better understand, or wants to be sure they got right the first time, and they are trying to figure it out. And that leads to the central feature of research—it is driven by a specific question. In a clever article entitled "10 Things Every Literacy Educator Should Know About Research," Duke and Martin (2011) provide this simple definition: "Research is the systematic collection and analysis of data to address a question" (11). That's it—a systematic approach to answering a question about how literacy works. This can include questions such as the following:

- Does invented spelling help children decode or spell words? Or can it be detrimental to their progress?
- Do students comprehend better if they are taught one comprehension strategy at a time?
- Do students learn letters best if they are carefully and thoroughly taught one letter per week?
- How should educators teach high-frequency words if students do not yet know the letter-sound patterns?

Research starts with a question, but good research is driven by the scientific method, a systematic approach to discovering how the world works. Science answers questions by setting up tests and observing results, or data. Scientific inquiry provides a specific way to answer questions.

Let's look at one of the questions above. Imagine you wanted to answer the question "Do students comprehend better if they are taught one comprehension strategy at a time or two or more strategies at a time?" One way to address this question might be to talk to expert teachers and ask their opinions. Another way might be to reflect on your own experiences and think about what students liked, what they thought worked. Although both of these strategies might provide helpful and informed opinions, they would not be the kind of scientific research that really tests what works with students. To truly research the answer to this question, you would need to apply an instructional approach and test it out systematically. This is called *empirical research*, meaning that its claims are based on actually observing and collecting data to answer a question. This is different from using theories, tradition, hypotheses, or opinions to answer a question.

Empirical research related to the question about comprehension strategies would involve clearly describing two or more approaches that you want to test: (a) teaching one comprehension strategy at a time and (b) teaching two or more strategies at a time. Then, you would randomly assign two different groups of students to either approach A or approach B. After a period of time, you would assess each group on their comprehension to see which approach worked best. Of course, for this discussion, we have simplified the process. Conducting research is not always that simple, but the general idea is that empirical research starts with a question and then sets about answering that question in systematic ways.

In this book, we focus on quantitative studies and, in particular, (a) experimental studies; (b) correlational studies; and (c) meta-analyses, which pull together the results of many experiments (see a description in the next section). Experiments are like the example comparing the two approaches to comprehension strategy instruction.

Scientific experiments are designed to tell researchers whether one thing (a certain type of instruction) causes another thing (learning). Duke and Martin describe experiments in the following way:

> Researchers typically identify a focus, such as the use of a particular instructional approach, and measure its outcomes. Researchers attempt to eliminate alternative explanations for outcomes by creating groups of participants who differ in only one way—for example, in receiving or not receiving a particular instructional approach. (2011, 15)

One of the key features of experimental studies is that students are randomly assigned to the different approaches being tested (see figure 0.1). When you randomly assign students, it rules out any bias that would influence the results. For example, if researchers wanted to prove that learning two or more comprehension strategies at a time was best, they might assign the most skillful teachers to that technique or place the best readers in that group. This biased assignment of students to instructional approaches would mean that the results could be due to something other than the use of comprehension strategies—student or teacher skills.

Figure 0.1

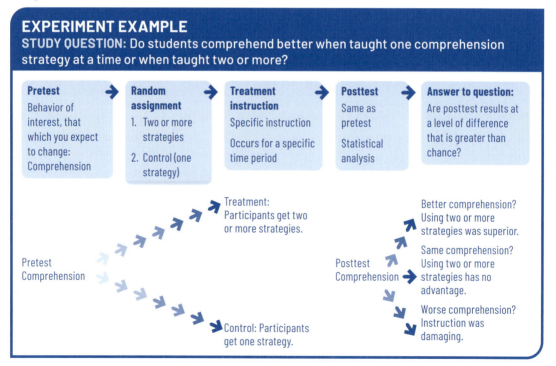

Correlational studies are those in which researchers examine relationships between naturally occurring variables (see figure 0.2). Researchers do correlational studies when they want to test relationships between variables and they cannot randomly assign study participants to different conditions. For example, imagine that researchers want to understand the impact of the amount of parent-child language in the home on vocabulary knowledge. They believe that more parent-child language is associated with better child vocabulary. It is not possible to randomly assign some children to parents who have high levels of oral exchanges and some to those who do not. Instead, researchers must measure the parent-child language in the home and child vocabulary knowledge and then look for relationships.

The relationship between variables is expressed mathematically in a correlation. Correlations range from 1.0 to -1.0, with positive correlations showing that as one variable goes up (e.g., parent-child language), the other variable goes up (e.g., vocabulary). If researchers found a strong positive relationship between parent-child language and vocabulary, they might draw the conclusion that language and vocabulary are related. However, they could not say that language *caused* vocabulary increases because they did not randomly assign children and there could be other influences on vocabulary that they did not capture (e.g., preschool experience, teacher-child ratios in childcare).

Figure 0.2

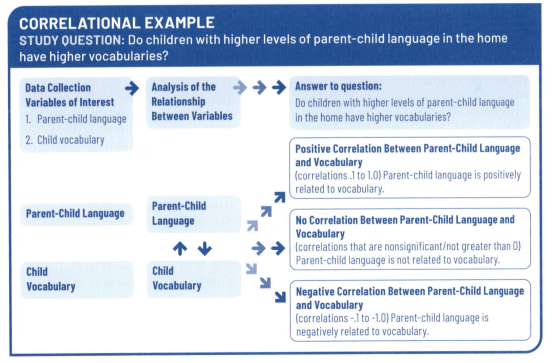

INTRODUCTION ▶▶▶ 5

Research Is Cumulative: Findings Strengthen When Separate Studies Repeatedly Show the Same Results

As challenging as it is to conduct even one study, we know that one study is not enough to inform what we do in a classroom. To apply something in the classroom, we need an accumulation of findings across many different research studies. When findings stack up and point to a pattern, we can really trust that we have results that can help teachers.

Replication is the repetition of a specific study using the same procedures. It is another very important part of the research process. Replication is repeating an experiment, either exactly or with modifications, to see if it gets the same results. A finding is trustworthy when researchers have repeatedly run the same tests on different samples and gotten the same results. Often, however, the results will differ between studies. While these differences can be puzzling on the surface, digging into how the studies were designed often leads to illuminating instructional insights.

When we analyze and compare research studies in terms of (1) **student characteristics** (age and abilities); (2) **assessment measures** (researcher-created or standardized measures); and (3) **intervention design** (duration or length, combination of instructional elements or strategies, whole-group versus small-group instruction), we can begin to develop a nuanced, sophisticated understanding of Science of Reading instruction (Shanahan 2020). This not only involves understanding the *what* of teaching reading but also informs teachers on the *when, for how long, for whom,* and the *why* of these evidence-based practices.

To consolidate findings, researchers use a technique called *meta-analysis*, which involves searching for studies addressing the same question(s) and then pooling the results of the studies statistically (see figure 0.3). A meta-analysis is a "study of studies," so to speak. The data in a meta-analysis are results from experimental and quasi-experimental studies. A meta-analysis will identify the average impact of a particular approach, not just from one study but across many studies. The accumulation of findings across research studies results in larger sample sizes and evidence collected across diverse contexts and conditions. The robustness of data collection leads to more confidence in the outcomes. Many of the questions in this book have been addressed by meta-analyses. (For a quick refresher on research study designs and effect sizes, we recommend the article "Effect Size Basics: Understanding the Strength of a Program's Impact" (wested.org/resources/rel-west-effect-size-basics-infographic).)

Figure 0.3

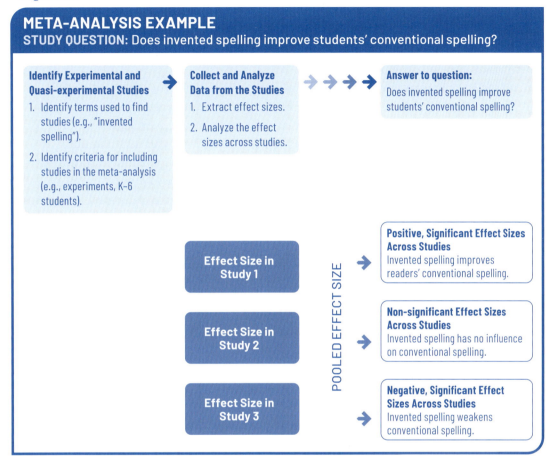

Research Is Not Always a Straight Path

In K–12 teacher education, we are sometimes so concerned with establishing research as our most important guiding principle in instructional decision-making that we forget that research continues to evolve. Einstein is famously credited with making the following statement: "If we knew what it was we were doing, it would not be called research, would it?" And this is the truth. We all know only what we know right now. Every finding is only as good as the last study. Science, by its very nature, is constantly evolving. Our understanding, indeed our scientific theories, are constantly being reshaped as our knowledge accumulates through research over time. This means that science is "provisional and cumulative" and that "both aspects are to be valued. They reveal not the weakness of science but its greatest strength" (Malik 2020, para. 5). We were recently reminded of this when we listened to a well-known science podcast and learned that the understanding of how planets are formed has completely changed since we went to elementary school! If the understanding of how our solar system was created has changed so fundamentally, little wonder then that the understanding of how reading happens is also still developing.

It used to be that research showed that planets formed when rocks and material in space violently collided. We still remember watching depictions of these violent collisions in science class! However, observations and data from more recent spacecraft have shifted astronomers' theories of how planets form. It is now understood that planets form by the gradual accumulation or fusion of rocks and material in space. This is science at its best. Theories provide frameworks of explanations and predictions of phenomena. They are meant to be testable and are dynamic. Researchers modify theories as additional research supports or contradicts them. Just as physical and medical theories continue to evolve, so too do educational theories, including understanding about reading development and instruction. This means that the Science of Reading is not a "settled science."

It is important to note that there is no one mega-theory that explains all there is to know about reading. If there were, there would be no reason to continue to do research. Rather, different theories illuminate different aspects of reading. The Simple View of Reading (Gough and Tunmer 1986) is often synonymous with the Science of Reading in many teachers' minds. The Simple View of Reading is a useful model that captures the critical roles of decoding and linguistic comprehension in reading comprehension. In the Simple View of Reading, reading is a product of decoding, defined as the ability to "read isolated words quickly, accurately and silently," and listening or linguistic comprehension (Gough and Tunmer 1986, 7). In the original model, these two factors were independent. Thus, both factors were necessary components, and a weakness in one or both would lead to a weakness in reading. Many teachers are also familiar with Scarborough's Rope model of reading (2001), which unpacked the word recognition (associated with decoding) and language comprehension components associated with the Simple View of Reading. In this model, the word recognition strand consists of three components:

- phonological awareness (which includes phonemic awareness)
- decoding
- sight recognition

The language comprehension strand is made up of the following components:

→ background knowledge
→ vocabulary
→ language structures
→ verbal reasoning
→ literacy knowledge

Figure 0.4. Active View of Reading Model (Duke and Cartwright 2021)

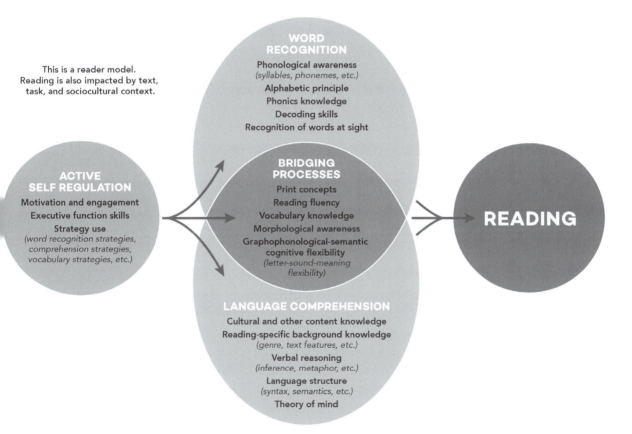

Reprinted from "The Science of Reading Progresses: Communicating Advances Beyond the Simple View of Reading," by N. K. Duke and K. B. Cartwright, 2021, *Reading Research Quarterly*, 56 (S1), S25-S44. © 2021 The Authors. Reprinted with permission.

Since Scarborough's Rope model was published, over two additional decades of research have informed our understanding of the key factors that predict reading comprehension. The Active View of Reading (Duke and Cartwright 2021) is a recent addition that includes many of the same components in Scarborough's Rope, along with the addition of active self-regulation and bridging processes that capture the overlap between word recognition and language comprehension. These bridging processes include print concepts, reading fluency, vocabulary knowledge, morphological awareness, and graphophonological-semantic cognitive flexibility. The model also calls attention to the contribution that cultural knowledge has on language comprehension. (See figure 0.4 below for a visual summary of the Active View of Reading.) These models or theories of reading are useful in their ability to predict why students struggle with reading and also their ability to point to effective interventions to remediate these difficulties. We particularly like the Active View of Reading because of its comprehensive nature and how it depicts relationships between the components. As with all theories, new research is beginning to test it (Burns, Duke, and Cartwright 2023); see Question 18 (page 153) on executive function skills for more information.

The evolving nature of science and research means that those who translate research are constantly trying to stay ahead of the curve by reading new studies that come out. Unfortunately, as soon as a research study or translational book like this one comes out, other pieces will produce new findings and revisions. We offer this as a caution to the reader that this volume represents our understanding of reading developing and instruction based on available research at the time of publication. We fully expect—and indeed, look forward to—new research to push forward what we know about the field of reading.

Inside This Book

We designed this book to answer common questions in a way that is practical for busy classroom teachers. We want a teacher to be able to spot a question in the table of contents, flip to the section addressing that question, read the section, and walk away with a clear understanding of how the research answers the question.

As teachers, we often teach our students how to preview an informational text using its text features. We teach that good readers preview a text to prepare to engage in that reading. For example, we may turn headings into questions or think about what we already know related to graphics or terms in boldface. Good readers also preview the text structure to get a sense of its overall organization. In fact, the topic of text-structure instruction is the subject of one of the focal questions in this book. In order to help you, the reader, navigate this book, we used a consistent organization system for each chapter, which makes your time with this text more efficient.

The book is organized around frequently asked question that we hear from teachers. We open each chapter with a discussion based on teaching elementary-level students to contextualize the question. We then offer some background knowledge to help you digest the discussion of research that follows. This background knowledge may include an explanation of key terms or a quick review of what we know from previous research.

Next you will find a list of the focal research citations that we used to answer the question. Reading research is so rich that it is impossible to cite all the relevant studies in a short summary. Instead, we have chosen a few key pieces of research related to each question that have direct implications for the K–5 classroom. We have identified focal research studies for an important reason. In many professional books that we read, it is often unclear which citations are for actual research studies and which are references that provide instructional recommendations (e.g., a *Reading Teacher* article with recommendations based on research). We want you to know which articles report on research that directly studied the focal question.

Following the list of focal research studies, we summarize their key findings— what we learned from the research. Finally, we arrive at the "So What? Actions for the Classroom" section, where we offer practical, actionable instructional recommendations for the K–5 classroom based on the focal research.

In addition, most questions include "Other Useful Resources," a section that offers teaching resources related to the question. And because literacy research is still evolving and not settled, we offer caveats at the end of several of the questions, cautioning the reader in interpreting the research and pointing out questions that still have limited answers.

See pages 12 and 13 for diagrams that show how the questions are set up. The consistent format makes it easy to skip around to sections that will help you the most in the moment. In fact, we encourage dipping and diving through the text based on the needs of your students! The goal of the book is to entertain your own curiosity, cutting to questions that you care about the most.

Question Organization

Question: The classroom-based question being examined.

Discussion from the Classroom: Common concerns that teachers voice about the question. Why answering the question is important for classroom practice.

Background and Assumptions: Established facts, theories, or ideas. Definitions.

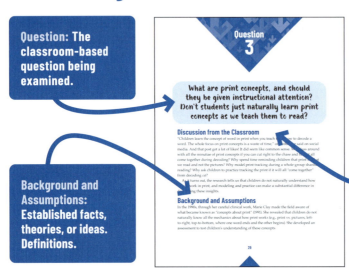

Research Studies That Inform the Question: List of citations for studies that best answer the question. Often these include meta-analyses. These studies are the bases for answering the question.

Research Findings: Translation of findings from cited studies. Main themes listed as subheadings.

So What? Actions for the Classroom: Actionable steps or instructional choices based on the findings.

Other Useful Resources: Additional articles, how-to pieces, or theories about the topic, often not research.

Translational Graphics: Graphic that lists the main classroom applications of the findings along with the citations.

INTRODUCTION >>> 13

PART 1

Foundational Skills That Support

WORD RECOGNITION

Question 1

I know that "letter of the week" is not the way to go, but how many letters should I teach per week?

Discussion from the Classroom

Most teachers know that the tradition of teaching one letter per week is not effective (Sunde, Furnes, and Lundetræ 2020). Here are some of the reasons that teaching this way is not the best idea for students:

1. It is too slow. There are twenty-six letters and thirty-six weeks in the typical school year. If you teach only one letter per week, students do not know all the letter sounds until about April.
2. Not all letters require a full week. Some letters children already know. In fact, most children will know the letters at the beginning of the alphabet as well as some of the letters in their name (Drouin, Horner, and Sondergeld 2012; Phillips et al. 2012). Why teach letters children know? And why spend a week on Aa if everyone already knows it?
3. Not everyone needs the same amount of letter instruction. In one study, kindergartners knew between one and fifty-two letters (Phillips et al. 2012), meaning that children did not all need the same letter instruction, a point made by other researchers (Stahl 1998; Treiman 2000).
4. Not all letters present the same level of difficulty for learners (Drouin, Horner, and Sondergeld 2012). Some are harder and need more time, and others are easier and need less time.

Of course, teachers, being the pragmatic professionals that they are, always ask, "Okay, so if one letter per week is too few, then what number is right? How many letters *should* I teach per week? What does the research say?" Three studies specifically addressed different rates of letter introduction to learners (Jones and Reutzel 2012; Sunde, Furnes, and Lundetræ 2020; Vadasy and Sanders 2021).

Background and Assumptions

Many teachers are familiar with the term *letter,* but fully understanding how an alphabetic system works requires understanding the more technical terms *phoneme* and *grapheme.* Below are brief definitions of these terms:

→ **Phoneme.** A *phoneme* is a speech sound, the smallest unit of sound in a language that differentiates meaning. For example, the words *cat* and *cot* differ by one speech sound, *a/o,* and that difference distinguishes the words' meanings (e.g., *animal* vs. *small bed*).

→ **Letter.** A *letter* is a unit in an alphabetic writing system that usually represents just one phoneme or speech sound. Letters combine to form words. There are two types of letters, consonants and vowels, representing phonemes formed in a variety of ways.

→ **Grapheme.** Within the context of literacy research and instruction, a *grapheme* is the written expression of a phoneme made up of one or more letters. In English there are 26 letters but about 44 phonemes; to represent all the phonemes, some graphemes combine letters. (e.g., *beat, toil, bark*).

Research Studies That Inform the Question

Jones, C. D., and D. R. Reutzel. 2012. "Enhanced Alphabet Knowledge Instruction: Exploring a Change of Frequency, Focus, and Distributed Cycles of Review." *Reading Psychology* 33 (5): 448–464.

Sunde, K., B. Furnes, and K. Lundetræ. 2020. "Does Introducing the Letters Faster Boost the Development of Children's Letter Knowledge, Word Reading and Spelling in the First Year of School?" *Scientific Studies of Reading* 24 (2): 141–158.

Vadasy, P. F., and E. A. Sanders. 2021. "Introducing Grapheme-Phoneme Correspondences (GPCs): Exploring Rate and Complexity in Phonics Instruction for Kindergartners with Limited Literacy Skills." *Reading and Writing* 34: 109–138.

Research Findings ⬅⬅⬅⬅

An Average of Three Graphemes per Week Resulted in Better Learning, Especially for Lower Skilled and Multilingual Learners

In our opinion, an experimental study by Vadasy and Sanders (2021) provides the most helpful guidance on how many letters to introduce per week. Researchers identified kindergarten and first grade students, including multilingual learners, who did not have high levels of letter knowledge and randomly assigned them to one of the following groups:

1. Slow: five weeks of instruction in ten letters, two per week
2. Fast: five weeks of instruction in fifteen letters, three per week

Interestingly, these researchers did not simply teach single-letter graphemes but also taught some multi-letter units. All students were taught the graphemes *a*, *m*, *ea*, *s*, *t*, *oo*, *d*, *o*, *sh*, and *r*, and students in the Fast group were also taught *n*, *ai*, *g*, and *ck*. After five weeks, researchers tested students on (a) letter names (taught); (b) letter sounds (taught); (c) letter spellings (taught); (d) word reading (consonant-vowel-consonant [cvc]); and (e) spelling (cvc). Students in the Fast group had learned more graphemes. This study suggests that at-risk kindergarten and first grade students, as well as students who are multilingual learners, learn more graphemes when taught three per week.

Teachers Who Introduce All Letters Earlier in the Year Positively Impact Learning, Especially for Lower Skilled and Multilingual Learners

A study in Norway examined natural differences that teachers reported in rates of letter introduction across the school year (Sunde, Furnes, and Lundetræ 2020). This was not an experimental study, and there was no random assignment to different rates of instruction. Researchers examined the impact that different rates of letter instruction had on over 900 children's (a) letter knowledge; (b) word-reading accuracy; (c) sight-word efficiency; and (d) spelling after a year.

Students took tests on the four measures at the beginning and end of the year, and researchers used a teacher survey to identify their rate of letter instruction. The main question on the survey was, "By the end of which month did you complete the first introduction of the letters?"

Children who learned letters at faster paces performed best on all measures (letter knowledge, word reading, sight word, and spelling). This was especially true for the lowest performing children and for multilingual learners. About 50 percent of teachers introduced all letters by December. If students learn letters earlier, they may have more time for repetition and practice, more time to learn how to *apply* letter-knowledge to decoding and spelling, and more time with the harder letters. Essentially, there is a timesaving efficiency that benefits students.

We want to provide a few caveats and clarifications about this study. In the study, the mean age of children at school entry was about 6.5 years, making them at least one year older than most kindergartners in the United States. In addition, the Norwegian language is more regular than English, meaning there are fewer "exception" words (e.g., *said, of, enough*).

Repeated Letter Cycles with One Letter per Day and Formative Assessment Resulted in Fewer At-Risk Students

In a two-year longitudinal study, researchers tested the impact of what they called Enhanced Alphabet Knowledge (EAK) instruction in comparison to traditional instruction (Jones and Reutzel 2012). This was not an experimental study; students were not randomly assigned instructional treatments. Instead, each teacher used either EAK or traditional instruction. EAK instruction included the following: (a) letter-a-day pacing with increasing flexibility; (b) distributed review cycles; and (c) lessons that efficiently teach students alphabet knowledge. Distributed review is review that takes place over a longer period and, in this study, formed 10 to 20 percent of the instructional time. The study took place in four urban schools, with nine teachers and over two hundred students using EAK and four teachers and ninety-two students using a traditional approach in Year 1.

Based on the Letter Naming Fluency measure of the Dynamic Indicators of Basic Early Literacy Skills (DIBELS), the study showed that by the end of the first year, EAK instruction reduced the number of at-risk students and increased the number of students meeting the benchmark. EAK instruction was 1.5 times more effective at reducing risk and 2.9 times more effective at helping students meet the benchmark. The EAK instruction was multidimensional, and all three elements of it—review, formative assessment, one letter per day—contributed to its effectiveness.

So What? Actions for the Classroom

Teach Three to Five Letters per Week, with All Letters Introduced by December

Together, the three studies offered several big takeaways. First, learners, including multilingual and at-risk learners, learned more when their teachers presented three to five letters per week. In another study, teachers who introduced all the letters by December saw more growth. This is interesting because teachers' instincts often say to slow down with learners who are struggling, but in the case of letters, slower was not better. Of course, the details of the letter instruction are important. Fast, sloppy teaching will not be effective, and just going fast is not the only ingredient. So, in following a pace of three to five letters per week, make sure to follow the additional research-based suggestions.

Teach Letters in Assessment-Informed Cycles with Predictable Routines

A study of letter cycles showed that after presenting all the letters, teachers assessed students to see which letters needed more time and for which students. Then they taught those specific letters to students who needed to learn them. Their pacing and selection of content was driven by responsive instruction. Simply reteaching content without assessment is inefficient and wastes instructional time. The teaching routine was clear and simply asked students to identify the letter name and sound, recognize the letter in text, and write the letter.

Use Distributed Review

The research on practice tells us that distributed review over days is better than longer practice sessions that take place less frequently. The most successful letter instruction used 10 to 20 percent of the instructional time to practice letters recently learned while also reviewing some that were learned less recently. It can take four to six weeks for some content to really stick. In addition, with a short, daily practice session reviewing previous letters, a teacher can quickly reteach or emphasize content that may have "slipped" over a break or a long weekend. So, teach a bit faster, but also review systematically each day using about 10 to 20 percent of the instructional time. Keep the practice uncomplicated and offer each child many opportunities to identify letter sounds.

For a graphic that shows the answer to this chapter's question, turn the page!

How many letters should I teach per week?

Three to five letters per week

In an experimental study, at-risk and multilingual learners learned more with a three-letters-per-week routine.

In a study with multiple components, a pace of one letter per day resulted in more students meeting benchmarks in letter naming.

Review letters based on assessment

Teachers used assessments after teaching all letters to see which students needed more time for which letters.

Introduce all by December

In a longitudinal study, children whose teachers introduced all letters by December learned more—this was especially true for at-risk and multilingual learners.

Distributed Review 10% to 20% of instructional time

At-risk and multilingual learners benefit from a faster pace.

(Jones and Reutzel 2012; Sunde, Furnes, and Lundetræ 2020; Vadasy and Sanders 2021)

Question 2

Should I teach letter names or letter sounds?

Discussion from the Classroom

With all the focus on following reading science, some teachers are confused about whether to teach letter names. Gladys, a teacher in an urban school, shared with us the following experience: "I was told by a presenter that teaching letter names did not reflect the Science of Reading. Is it wrong to teach children letter names along with letter sounds?" In 1997, McGuiness strongly advised teachers not to teach letter names, arguing that letter sounds were the essential information and that learning names could interfere with learning letter sounds (McGuiness 1997). At some level, she was right. In fact, in the United Kingdom, letter names are typically not taught first, because children need to know letter sounds when they decode words. When a reader comes to the word *big* in print, they do not decode it by naming the letters *b, i,* and *g*. Instead, they go right to the sounds, blending them /b/, /i/, /g/, *biiiiig, biiig, big,* until they recognize the word as one they know. More recently, Dehaene, author of *Reading in the Brain* (2009), made a similar claim about letter names. Heidi Anne has had concerns herself about an overemphasis on teaching letter names, especially in preschools. In fact, it motivated her to write a blog post entitled "Naming letters is not a straight path to literacy: Here's why."

Is teaching children letter names useful? Necessary? Harmful? Neither? Fortunately, a series of research studies have addressed these questions quite well, although the evidence is not completely conclusive. But the patterns are clear.

Background and Assumptions

Have you ever had a kindergartner tell you that Ww shows the /d/ sound? Or write the word *why* as *Y*? Children do this because many letters (clearly not Ww or Yy) have their letter sound in their name. For example, the letter Bb's main sound is represented by the letter at the beginning of the letter name ("Bee"). This is called an "acrophonic" letter, meaning the name of the letter starts with the letter itself and the target sound represented.

In letters like Ff, the main speech sound represented by the letter is at the end of the letter name ("Eff"). Even the vowels carry their long or tense sound in their names (Aa as in *ate*) but not their short or lax sound (Aa as in *apple*). The letters Cc and Gg have the soft sounds at the beginning of their names, but not the more common hard sounds, as in *cat* and *go*. A small group of letter names do not possess letter-sound information in them at all (e.g., Hh, Yy, Ww). Thus, well over half of letter names have letter-sound information in them.

Letter Name/Letter Sounds Relationship	Letters	Letter Names
Acrophonic Letters: Letter names with sound information at the beginning of the name	Bb, Dd, Jj, Kk, Pp, Tt, Vv, Zz	"**B**ee," "**D**ee," "**J**ay," "**K**ay," "**P**ea," "**T**ee," "**V**ee," "**Z**ee"
Non-Acrophonic Letters: Letter names with sound information at the end of the name	Ff, Ll, Mm, Nn, Rr, Ss, Xx	"E**ff**," "E**ll**" "E**m**" "E**n**" "A**re**" "E**s**" "E**x**"
Partial Information: Letter names that have partial sound information in the name	Cc, Gg, Qq	Qq can represent the /k/ sound in words like *unique*, but more commonly represents a consonant cluster (/kw/). Cc and Gg have both soft and hard sounds, with the letter name reflecting the soft sounds.
Vowels: (Long or tense sound information only)	Aa, Ee, Ii, Oo, Uu	
No Information: Letter names without sound information	Hh, Ww, Yy	"Aych" "Double u" "Why"

Research Studies That Inform the Question

Ellefson, M. R., R. Treiman, and B. Kessler. 2009. "Learning to Label Letters by Sounds or Names: A Comparison of England and the United States." *Journal of Experimental Child Psychology* 102 (3): 323–341.

Piasta, S. B., D. J. Purpura, and R. K. Wagner. 2010. "Fostering Alphabet Knowledge Development: A Comparison of Two Instructional Approaches." *Reading and Writing: An Interdisciplinary Journal* 23 (6): 607–626.

Roberts, T. A., P. F. Vadasy, and E. A. Sanders. 2018. "Preschoolers' Alphabet Learning: Letter Name and Sound Instruction, Cognitive Processes, and English Proficiency." *Early Childhood Research Quarterly* 44: 257–274.

Share, D. L. 2004. "Knowing Letter Names and Learning Sounds: A Causal Connection." *Journal of Experimental Child Psychology* 88 (3): 213–233.

Research Findings

With Some Phonemic Awareness, Children Use Letter Names to Help Them Learn Many Letter Sounds

Believe it or not, some studies show that teaching letter names helps with letter-sound learning. Most studies suggest that letter names can provide some advantages when learning letter sounds. In one experiment, children were asked to learn the names of made-up letter forms that were created for the purposes of the experiment to ensure that children did not already know them (Share 2004). Group 1 learned letter names that were acrophonic and Group 2 learned letters that were not (e.g., "The letter *sheb* represents the sound /sh/ vs. *grack* represents the sound /w/"). After learning letter names, each group was taught sounds, and predictably, Group 1 performed the best, using the letter names to learn corresponding letter sounds. However, the researchers found that, in order to use the sound information in the letter name, children had to have some awareness of phonemes at the beginning of words. If they could not tell, for example, that the words *bean* and *banana* both started with /b/, then they could not use the letter-name/letter-sound connection.

A similar experiment also suggested that not just children but also adults benefited from using information contained in letter names to learn sounds (Treiman, Sotak, and Bowman 2001). Still other nonexperimental research has examined patterns in letter knowledge to see if there were differences in children's letter-sound knowledge for the different types of letter names described above (Treiman et al. 2008). As it turned out, there were! Even children with language disorders and speech impairments performed better on the acrophonic letters (e.g., Tt, Vv) than they performed on letter sounds with information at the end of the name (e.g., Ss, Ff) or no helpful information in the name (e.g., Hh, Yy). In contrast to the Share (2004) study, these researchers also measured phonemic and phonological awareness and did not find them to relate to children's abilities to use letter names to extrapolate letter-sound information.

One study did not support the pattern of acrophonic letter sounds being learned more easily. Researchers in that study taught preschoolers acrophonic letter names and non-acrophonic names and did not find that children learned the sounds for acrophonic letters better (Roberts, Vadasy, and Sanders 2018).

In the United States, Research Supports Learning Names and Sounds Together

In 2009, researchers conducted a very interesting study titled "Learning to Label Letters by Sounds or Names: A Comparison of England and the United States" (Ellefson, Treiman, and Kessler 2009). The study found that US children knew more letter names and English children knew more letter sounds. (No surprise there! Kids learn what we teach them.) Eventually those differences faded. In addition, children in both countries tended to use the letter name or sound information that they knew to bootstrap or learn information that they did not know. So, English children used letter sounds to learn names (e.g., "The sound for Bb is /b/ so the name must be Bee.") and US children used letter names to learn letter sounds ("The sound for this letter must be /b/ because it is the sound I hear at the beginning of Bb.").

Another experimental study randomly assigned preschoolers to learning either (a) letter names and sounds together or (b) just letter sounds (Piasta, Purpura, and Wagner 2010). The children learning both letter names and sounds performed best. In a similar experiment, researchers randomly assigned students to one of four instructional treatments: (a) letter names only; (b) letter sounds only; (c) letter names and sounds (with additional elements); and (d) "business as usual" control group (Roberts, Vadasy, and Sanders 2018). The study showed that, even for the dual-language learners in the study (about 30 percent of participants), the combination of learning letter names and letter sounds led to higher-than-average growth. In addition, researchers found that learning letter sounds only was more challenging.

So What? Actions for the Classroom

Present Both Letter Names and Sounds from the Start

In the United States, there is a tradition of teaching young children letter names. Many preschoolers are frequently exposed to letter names prior to formal schooling through books, games, and software. Most preschool assessments and benchmarks feature letter names, and the Head Start Early Learning Outcomes does as well. This is not a research-based practice. However, given the exposure that many children will have to letter names, and the research that tells us that children will use what they know about letter names to learn the sounds, it makes sense to pair letter names and sounds when introducing letters to children. Teaching letter names is useful and does not hurt students. The research suggests letter names can help children learn sounds. As the table on page 24 suggests, for over half of the letters, the names provide information that supports learning letter sounds.

Below are some basic steps to presenting both letters and sounds.

1. Present the letter in isolation along with a simple photo of an easily recognizable item that starts with the sound.
2. Say the sound in isolation, making sure not to add an extra "uh" sound.
3. Show the handwriting strokes and ask students to "air write." (Make sure to practice handwriting with a pencil and paper at another time.)
4. Name other items that start with the same sound.

Keep in mind that younger preschool students will most likely acquire the letter names first, but don't give up with the sounds. During review, add the sound: "Yes, that is the letter Tt. It spells the sound /t/." Get in the habit of asking "What sound?" right after children name the letter. Demonstrate how we use letters by conducting shared readings for print referencing and interactive writing to apply letter sounds.

Couple Letter Instruction with Phonemic Awareness

The research on letter names indicates that in order for students to use sound information in the names, they must be phonemically aware. This means that it is important to teach phonemic awareness alongside, before, during, and after letter instruction. For example, if you are teaching Bb, Tt, Aa, do some phonemic awareness work with those sounds (e.g., Bobby likes balls, bean, bows; sorting pictures by the beginning sound). Then, right after the phonemic work, show the letter with the sound (e.g., "If Bobby likes balls, beans, and bows, what letter does he need?"). Emphasize the beginning sounds in letter names (e.g., "Bb /bbbb/ Do you hear that Bb, /b/? The Bb starts with /b/."). Even follow up a lesson with "spelling" a sound (e.g., "Okay, so

I want to write about our turtle, Tonya. How do I spell that? Which letter spells that first sound?"). Often, phonemic awareness instruction takes place by itself in a separate part of the day where children practice rhyming or syllables. It's very important to embed phonemic awareness with letter instruction; the two work together. Emphasize the sounds in letter names, and do phonemic awareness activities with the sounds that match the lesson's target letters.

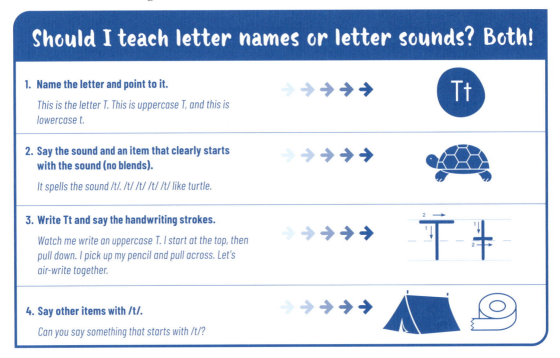

Other Useful Resources

Roberts, T. A. 2021. "Learning Letters: Evidence and Questions from a Science-of-Reading Perspective." *Reading Research Quarterly* **56: S171–S192.**

Question 3

What are print concepts, and should they be given instructional attention? Don't students just naturally learn print concepts as we teach them to read?

Discussion from the Classroom

"Children learn the concept of word in print when you teach them how to decode a word. The whole focus on print concepts is a waste of time," one educator said on social media. And that post got a lot of likes! It did seem like common sense. Why fuss around with all the minutiae of print concepts if you can cut right to the chase and have it all come together during decoding? Why spend time reminding children that print is what we read and not the pictures? Why model print tracking during a whole-group shared reading? Why ask children to practice tracking the print if it will all "come together" from decoding *cat*?

As it turns out, the research tells us that children do not naturally understand how words work in print, and modeling and practice can make a substantial difference in developing these insights.

Background and Assumptions

In the 1990s, through her careful clinical work, Marie Clay made the field aware of what became known as "concepts about print" (1991). She revealed that children do not naturally know all the mechanics about how print works (e.g., print vs. pictures, left-to-right, top-to-bottom, where one word ends and the other begins). She developed an assessment to test children's understanding of these concepts.

Within the collection of concepts about print, the specific insight about how words work is pivotal. This is called "concept of word in print." Researchers theorize that before they fully acquire and learn how to use letter sounds, children do not really know how to find the boundaries of words (Morris et al. 2003). They tend to treat a sentence as one continuous object, rather than composed of multiple word objects. It appears that children do not use the letter sounds or pay attention to the spaces between words.

Research Studies That Inform the Question

Ehri, L. C., and J. Sweet. 1991. "Fingerpoint Reading of Memorized Text: What Enables Beginners to Process the Print?" *Reading Research Quarterly* 26 (4): 442–462.

Evans, M. A., and J. Saint-Aubin. 2005. "What Children Are Looking at During Shared Storybook Reading: Evidence from Eye Movement Monitoring." *Psychological Science* 16 (11): 913–920.

Farry-Thorn, M., and R. Treiman. 2022. "Prereaders' Knowledge About the Nature of Book Reading." *Reading and Writing* 35: 1933–1952.

Justice, L. M., A. S. McGinty, S. B. Piasta, J. N. Kaderavek, and X. Fan. 2010. "Print-Focused Read-Alouds in Preschool Classrooms: Intervention Effectiveness and Moderators of Child Outcomes." *Language, Speech, and Hearing Services in Schools* 41 (4): 504–520.

Justice, L. M., L. E. Skibbe, A. Canning, and C. Lankford. 2005. "Pre-schoolers, Print and Storybooks: An Observational Study Using Eye Movement Analysis." *Journal of Research in Reading* 28 (3): 229–243.

Mesmer, H. A., and T. O. Williams. 2015. "Examining the Role of Syllable Awareness in a Model of Concept of Word: Findings from Preschoolers." *Reading Research Quarterly* 50 (4): 483–497.

Morris, D., J. W. Bloodgood, R. G. Lomax, and J. Perney. 2003. "Developmental Steps in Learning to Read: A Longitudinal Study in Kindergarten and First Grade." *Reading Research Quarterly* 38 (3): 302–328.

Nevo, E., and V. Vaknin-Nusbaum. 2018. "Enhancing Language and Print-Concept Skills by Using Interactive Storybook Reading in Kindergarten." *Journal of Early Childhood Literacy* 18 (4): 545–569.

Research Findings ⬅⬅⬅⬅⬅

Understanding What a Word Is in Print Does Not "Come Naturally"

What are young children looking at when they are watching an adult read to them? Can children know letters and letter sounds but not understand what a word is in print? As it turns out, empirical research informs these two questions, and it tells us that insights about how words work are *not* natural (Farry-Thorn and Treiman 2022; Justice et al. 2005). Two eye movement studies show that pre-readers (ages three to five-and-a-half) do not naturally pay attention to words. In one study, children only looked at print, even when it was set apart by itself on a page, less than 10 percent of the time (Evans and Saint-Aubin 2005). Another study found that when children were watching and listening to a traditional picture book with very prominent pictures, they looked at the print only 2.7 percent of the time. Even when they were watching and listening to a specially constructed picture book with larger and more prominent print, they only fixated on print a maximum of 7 percent of the time. In fact, even children who had letter knowledge did not pay more attention to print (Justice et al. 2005).

Another study tested the behaviors of preschoolers (Farry-Thorn and Treiman 2022). The study measured the preschoolers' knowledge of letters and words beforehand and then tested the following questions: "Do pre-readers who can identify letters and words in a book understand that the print is the part of the book that is read?" The study presented children with different sets of facing text pages (i.e., one page on the left and one on the right). In each set, the page on the left had only pictures and page on the right had either a single letter or only words. Researchers asked the children to point to the page with the pictures, point to the page with the letter, and point to the page with the words. They found that 97 percent of preschoolers correctly pointed to the page with letters (but not words), and 94 percent correctly pointed to the page with words. But when asked, "Can you point to the page that I can read?" only 58 percent of the children pointed to the page with print. This showed that children could know the labels *letter* and *word*, and even know some actual letters, but still not conceptually understand how that relates to reading.

Children Develop Concept of Word in Predictable Patterns

How can we tell that children know where one printed word begins and another ends, and why is that even important? Researcher Morris and colleagues (2003) found that if you ask children to memorize a line of print and then watch them try to coordinate the words that they say as they point, you can understand their understanding of words. As children are learning letters and letter sounds, they also need to learn how to *use* that information in the acts of reading and writing. When young children look at a line of print and do not have alphabetic knowledge, it all blends together. An adult pays attention to the spaces between words as a way to find word boundaries and then, when reading, use the alphabetic information (e.g., "B" = /b/). The examples below are from the classic children's book *Brown Bear, Brown Bear, What Do You See?* by Bill Martin Jr.

Skilled Reader's View of a Line:	*Brown Bear, brown bear, what do you see?* eight words in a sentence about a bear
Young Child's View of a Line:	BxoxxBxxx,xoxxbxxx,xxoxxo? a line of visual symbols, many of which they don't know

Before children learn how to fully decode words like *brown* and *bear*, they learn some letter sounds and they start to understand the connection between the visual letter and sounds of speech. Early in their learning, at a stage called "pre-alphabetic," children will not use the letter-sound information to help them attempt to spell or read words. (Ehri and Sweet 1991). They might try to spell a word like *dog* using letters that they know (e.g., Stsst) or might try to remember a word based on its shape (e.g., *look* has two o's; *Tyrannosaurus* is long) but will not be able to identify the letter sounds. Once children learn letter sounds, they are partial alphabetic readers and can use that information in their attempts. For example, they can use the /b/ sound to help them know where the words *brown* and *bear* are (Morris et al. 2003). Eventually children learn all the letter-sound patterns so that they can fully decode words (e.g., b-r-ow-n).

There are three phases of concept of word in print, characterized by the degree to which children can match their voices to the visual words that they are pointing to (Mesmer and Williams 2015; Morris et al. 2003). The phases are as follows:

1. Beginning phase: random pointing that does not have a voice-to-print match. In this example, the child points to the word *brown* and says the whole line, instead of pointing to each word as he says it.

Print:	*Brown Bear, brown bear, what do you see?*
Pointing:	↑
Voice:	"Brown Bear, brown bear, what do you see?"

2. Second phase: pointing matches print inconsistently and often not for multisyllabic words. Notice the child is saying the second syllable of *yell-ow* while pointing to the word *duck*.

Print:	*I*	*see*	*a*	*yellow*	*duck*	*looking at*	*me.*	
Pointing:	↑	↑	↑	↑	↑	↑	↑	↑
Voice:	"I	see	a	yell ow	duck	look	ing" (ran out of text to point to)	

3. Final phase: Completely accurate voice-to-print match with multisyllabic words.

Print:	*I*	*see a*		*yellow*	*duck*	*looking*	*at*	*me.*
Pointing:	↑	↑ ↑	↑	↑		↑	↑	↑
Voice:	"I	see	a	yellow	duck	looking	at	me."

The development of concept of word in print fits into a broader developmental sequence in early literacy (Morris et al. 2003). Specifically, children use their burgeoning alphabetic knowledge as they acquire concept of word in print. According to the study, development occurred in the following steps: (1) naming letters; (2) becoming aware of beginning phonemes; (3) spelling beginning sound and demonstrating concept of word; (4) segmenting phonemes; (5) reading words; and (6) reading passages (Morris et al. 2003). Concept of word depends on knowledge of letter sounds, and it is a prerequisite for reading words and passages.

Teachers' Print Referencing During Shared Reading Improves Children's Understandings of Print Concepts

Many studies describe development, but that does not necessarily mean that instruction can or will influence development. Can we enhance children's insights about print and words with instruction? From the research, the answer is a resounding yes! A series of studies examining how teachers' print referencing affects children can guide classroom practice (Justice et al. 2010; Nevo and Vaknin-Nusbaum 2018).

First, we know that when teachers read books with large print aloud to children and point to that print in teacher-led instruction, children will attend to words and print much more than they will without teacher-led instruction (Justice et al. 2010). In a randomized control trial with fifty-nine teachers of four- and five-year-olds, teachers were assigned to read the same collection of books over thirty weeks under one of two conditions: (a) high-dose print referencing (e.g., teachers pointing to words, prompting, asking questions about print) and (b) comparison group (e.g., read the same book on the same schedule using business-as-usual reading style). Children in the print-referencing group had higher measures on a composite measure of print awareness. The findings were a replication of an earlier study (Justice et al. 2009).

Another quasi-experiment examined a similar intervention with Hebrew-speaking children who were randomly assigned to one of two groups: an interactive shared reading group and a control group (Nevo and Vaknin-Nusbaum 2018). The interactive storybook reading taught print concepts along with language skills (morphology, vocabulary, and phonological awareness). The interactive reading impacted children's learning of print concepts, morphology, vocabulary, and phonological awareness. The study also found that children's pretest motivation influenced their learning of print concepts, pointing to the importance of engagement as children learn print concepts.

So What? Actions for the Classroom

Do Not Assume Students Conceptually Understand the Difference Between Letters, Words, and Sentences

The research demonstrates that many children do not naturally understand that letters make up words or even that words are the part that we "read." They see pictures as most useful and often just don't attend to print because it is not interpretable to them. How do you know if you are assuming that children understand these concepts, and how can you avoid making that assumption? First, although you must teach letter shapes and sounds using isolated letters, do not do this to the exclusion of modeling real reading. If children are always working with isolated letters and never see them being used in an extended text, they are unlikely to get "the big picture" (see procedures below). As obvious as it sounds, they will not connect letters with reading ("Oh, these letters are what we read") or understand that letters group together to form words. It's like teaching someone about all the different types of bolts that there are (e.g., bugle head, dome head, raised head) without telling them that they are building a ship!

Second, as you are teaching letters, give children time to acquire these insights about print. It does not happen overnight, and so you must keep the shared reading going as you are teaching letters. Third, as described below, rely on modeling and shared participation for building insights about how words work as much as you depend on direct explanation. Usually, direct explanation will not go as far in developing understandings as ongoing modeling and shared participation. The teaching of letters must be constantly integrated with learning how those letters work and why in the world you might learn them!

Teach Print Concepts During Shared Whole-Group Reading

There is a well-known piece of advice that fiction writers are given about developing a story: "Show, don't tell." This advice also applies to print concepts and concept of word.

We cannot just tell students how this all works, we must show them. If we could just tell students, "This is a letter, and letters are used to build words," then it would all be easy. But we are introducing children to something that they have never experienced before—a visual, written system that creates a code for the speech that they know. Concepts take time to develop and understand. In fact, Vygotsky explained, "Direct teaching of concepts is impossible and fruitless. A teacher who tries to do this usually accomplishes nothing but empty verbalism, a parrot-like repetition of words by the child, simulating a knowledge of the corresponding concepts but actually covering up a vacuum" (1986, 149–50). We can get students to parrot us and repeat back the phrases that we tell them, but that does not mean that they understand a concept.

In order to help children learn about print concepts particularly, use whole-group modeling with books or text projected onto a whiteboard so children can see the words. In fact, the words should be prominent, consistently placed on the page, and memorable to children. Below are four areas of print referencing (print organization, print meaning, letters, and words) and questions that teachers might use to draw attention to these areas.

Focus	Description	Questions/Prompts
Print Organization	page order, title, print organization (left-to-right), author	• "The author, Patricia Polacco, wrote the book" (points to author's name). • "Where should I start reading?" (top or bottom; left page or right page)
Print Meaning	you read print, environmental print, concept of reading	• "Where would I read the story?" • "Look, this writing on the can says *red paint*." • "These are the words Clem is saying" (pointing to a speech bubble).
Letters	letter sounds, uppercase vs. lowercase	• "Can you find a letter you know?" • "What sound should I say when I see this letter?" • "This is an uppercase Gg."
Words	letter vs. word, short vs. long, print tracking	• "Can you find a long word? It will have lots of letters." • "Let's point to just one letter." • "Can you point to the words while we say them? Look at the beginning of the words. Listen."

(Justice et al. 2009)

In addition to asking children questions in these areas, teachers can also use different techniques and vary the levels of support that they offer. Techniques might include modeling (e.g., "When I want to read the next word, I go this way" (point to the right)), using nonverbals along with verbal (e.g., point to the word *go* and say "go"), asking children to participate (e.g., "I am going to read this line, and Dillion is going to point to the words as I say them"), and explaining (e.g., "This is a speech bubble, and it shows the words the elephant is saying"). Teachers can also use high and low support (e.g., "I am going to read and point. Watch." vs. "Li Lin is going to come up here and point to the words and say them all by herself. Watch her.").

Print Tracking Develops Concept of Word in Print

Of all the print concepts, concept of word in print is one of the most important. This is where children *use* their burgeoning knowledge of letter sounds in a real application. As the research shows, children develop concept of word in print in stages by watching a teacher point to words in a line of memorized print and then doing it themselves.

Start with a predictable book with lines that are easy to memorize (e.g., *Brown Bear, Brown Bear What Do You See?*). The first time you read the book, do so without pointing or print-referencing instruction so that children can memorize the lines. The reason that children should memorize the lines is because they will not have the full knowledge of letter-sound patterns to decode the words. They are not "reading" really, just using a beginning sound and paying attention to word boundaries to track print. After children know the lines, demonstrate pointing to the print. Make sure that your pointing is *precise*. Do not point to any location on the word. Point to the beginning of the word, directly under the first letter, not blocking the letters with your fingers. Note that you will need to look at the print yourself to do this. Read slightly more slowly, pausing a bit to allow children time to process. Tell children, "Look at the words. Watch my finger." If children are not watching, they will get nothing from it.

As you model pointing over several days, you can try the following to challenge students:

→ "I would like a friend to come up and point to the words as we say them. Pay attention. Point to the words that we say."

→ "Watch me carefully, because I am going to try to trick you. Stop me if the word I am saying does not match the one I am pointing to." (Point to a word and say a different one. For example, "Brown fish. Is that right? No. It says *bear*. How do I know? That's not an Ff, that's a Bb, /b/.")

→ "Some words have two parts, but they are one word. Like *leap-ing, jump-ing*. When we point, we stay on the same word."

As children advance, they should be able to control their own pointing, especially with polysyllabic words. Do model this, however, by showing them that your finger stays on a polysyllabic word and does not move to the next word (e.g., "Look at when I say the word *moving*. It's long. I start at the *Mm* then stay on the word for both parts, *mov-ing*.").

Lastly, we suggest letting children do this themselves with small books that replicate the lines that the teacher modeled throughout the week. After doing whole-group instruction and asking individual children to demonstrate, give children their own individual books with the same story/rhyme/sentences and ask them to do it. We have used this in research with preschoolers (Mesmer and Lake 2010). Some educators and researchers discourage using individual books, because children are not actually decoding the words (Lindsey 2022). If that is your perspective, ask children to participate in a whole-group setting. The research does not point to individual books being either harmful or pivotal.

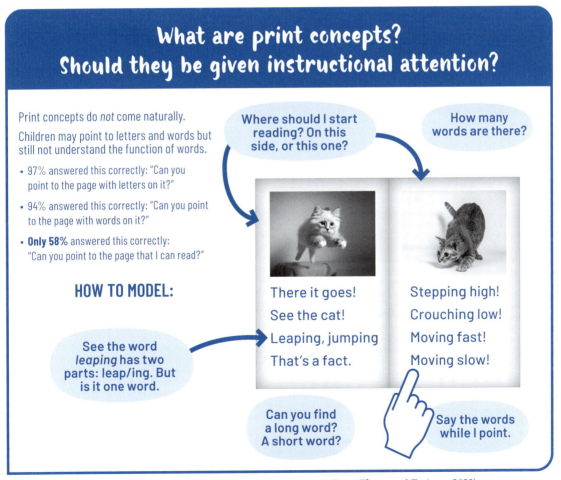

(Justice et al. 2009; Nevo and Vaknin-Nusbaum 2018; Farry-Thorn and Treiman 2022)

Other Useful Resources

Clay, M. M. 1989. "Concepts About Print in English and Other Languages." *The Reading Teacher* 42 (4): 268–276.

Justice, L. M., R. P. Bowles, and L. E. Skibbe. 2006. "Measuring Preschool Attainment of Print Concept Knowledge: A Study of Typical and At-Risk 3- to 5-Year-Old Children Using Item Response Theory." *Language, Speech, and Hearing Services in Schools* 37 (3): 224–235.

Justice, L. M., and H. K. Ezell. 2001. "Word and Print Awareness in 4-Year-old Children." *Child Language Teaching and Therapy* 17 (3): 207–225.

Justice, L. M., and H. K. Ezell. 2002. "Use of Storybook Reading to Increase Print Awareness in At Risk Children." *American Journal of Speech-Language Pathology* 11 (1): 17–29.

Justice, L. M., J. N. Kaderavek, X. Fan, A. Sofka, and A. Hunt. 2009. "Accelerating Preschoolers' Early Literacy Development Through Classroom-Based Teacher–Child Storybook Reading and Explicit Print Referencing." *Language, Speech, and Hearing Services in Schools* 40 (1): 67–85.

Mesmer, H. A. E., and K. Lake. 2010. "The Role of Syllable Awareness and Syllable-Controlled Text in the Development of Finger-Point Reading." *Reading Psychology* 31 (2): 176–201.

Mesmer, H. A., and T. O. Williams. 2015. "Examining the Role of Syllable Awareness in a Model of Concept of Word: Findings from Preschoolers." *Reading Research Quarterly* 50 (4): 483–497.

Question 4

Which phonological awareness skills are most important to teach, and how should I teach them?

Discussion from the Classroom

As the field is increasingly turning its attention toward dyslexia and embracing research-based practices, we are seeing more phonological awareness instruction in classrooms. But we have also witnessed a great deal of confusion about how much phonological awareness instruction students need and what that should look like. Teira, a teacher at a school in Texas, does a standalone phonological awareness program with her first graders for about ten minutes a day. The program covers many different sound units (e.g., syllables, words, onset/rime, phonemes) and uses many different tasks (e.g., blending, segmenting, deleting, manipulating). "I really like the program. It's fun, and there are a lot of hand motions for doing the activities. I just wonder if the kids need all of these different things. Like, toward the end, the kids have to take a sound off a word, replace it within another, and then say the new word. It is really hard, and I'm not sure if it is helping them." Teira's concern comes up a lot. Teachers want to know what the research says about all of the different sound units and task types in phonological awareness instruction.

Another common assertion that we have heard is that phonemic awareness instruction should always be done with letters, based on the National Reading Panel (NICHD 2000) report's statement that "PA [phonological awareness] instruction may be most effective when children are taught to manipulate phonemes with letters" (2-6). This one is challenging because, of course, the entire purpose of phonemic awareness is its application to decoding and spelling. Yet this kind of assertion leaves teachers worried about whether they should ever work with phonemes orally without letter tokens. Is it okay to use hand motions? What about pictures to conduct sound sorts that draw attention to initial sounds? Even with segmenting and blending words using Elkonin boxes, teachers wonder if they should always use letters as students push tokens into boxes.

Background and Assumptions

In the late 1990s, researchers discovered that in order for people to learn to read in an alphabetic language, they needed phonemic awareness. Phonemic awareness is the ability to recognize, identify, and manipulate individual sounds, or phonemes—speech sounds in a language. Phonemic awareness is distinct from phonics, which involves the relationship between letters and the sounds they represent. Phonemic awareness is an auditory skill, focusing on the sounds themselves rather than the written symbols. Phonemic awareness might include a student putting together the sounds of a word (e.g., "What is /g/ /a/ /p/?") or breaking the sounds of a word down (e.g., "What are the sounds in *ship*?"). Phonemic awareness is a pivotal skill in learning to read because the alphabetic symbols represent phonemes or speech sounds. If you learn the English code, you must understand that it is built on the individual sounds in words and not the syllables or whole words themselves.

Phonological awareness is insight about sound units of *any size* (e.g., words, syllables, onset-rime, phonemes). The purpose of working with sound units larger than the phoneme is to build capacity for phonemes, the units that are coded by letters. Researchers examined patterns in development and learned that children acquired awareness of larger sound units (e.g., words, syllables) before smaller units (e.g., phonemes) (Anthony et al. 2003). Both phonological and phonemic awareness are developed through different types of tasks such as these:

- segmenting units (e.g., ba-by, sh-i-p, h-at)
- blending units (e.g., ba-by = baby, sh-i-p = ship, h-at = hat)
- deleting units (e.g., "What is *baby* without 'bee'?")
- substituting (e.g., "Here's a word—*backbend*. What word do I have if I replace *bend* with *board*?").

This same research showed that receptive tasks were easier (e.g., "Point to the picture that starts with /p/") than productive tasks (e.g., "Tell me the sound at the beginning of *pig*"). Receptive tasks, from an oral language perspective, refer to tasks in which the child need only hear and demonstrate understanding, but need not produce a response expressively.

Research Studies That Inform the Question

Anthony, J. L., C. J. Lonigan, K. Driscoll, B. M. Phillips, and S. R. Burgess. 2003. "Phonological Sensitivity: A Quasi-Parallel Progression of Word Structure Units and Cognitive Operations." *Reading Research Quarterly* 38 (4): 470–487.

Ehri, L. C., S. R. Nunes, D. M. Willows, B. V. Schuster, Z. Yaghoub-Zadeh, and T. Shanahan. 2001. "Phonemic Awareness Instruction Helps Children Learn to Read: Evidence from the National Reading Panel's Meta-Analysis." *Reading Research Quarterly* 36 (3): 250-287.

Erbeli, F., M. Rice, Y. Xu, M. E. Bishop, and J. M. Goodrich. 2024. "A Meta-Analysis on the Optimal Cumulative Dosage of Early Phonemic Awareness Instruction." *Scientific Studies of Reading* 28 (4): 345–370.

Hulme, C., P. J. Hatcher, K. Nation, A. Brown, J. Adams, and G. Stuart. 2002. "Phoneme Awareness Is a Better Predictor of Early Reading Skill Than Onset-Rime Awareness." *Journal of Experimental Child Psychology* 82 (1): 2–28.

Kenner, B. B., N. P. Terry, A. H. Friehling, and L. L Namy. 2017. "Phonemic Awareness Development in 2.5- and 3.5-Year-Old Children: An Examination of Emergent, Receptive, Knowledge, and Skills." *Reading and Writing* 30: 1575–1594.

National Early Literacy Panel. 2008. *Developing Early Literacy: Report of the National Early Literacy Panel: A Scientific Synthesis of Early Literacy Development and Implications for Intervention.* National Institute for Literacy, National Center for Family Literacy. nichd.nih.gov/sites/default/files/publications/pubs/documents/NELPReport09.pdf.

Research Findings

Phonemic Awareness Instruction Contributes to Reading and Spelling

A finding that has continually been established in the literature is that phonemic awareness instruction—teaching children to recognize, identify, produce, and manipulate phonemes, or individual speech sounds—has a positive impact on reading and spelling (NICHD 2000). Pooling the results of fifty-two studies, researchers also identified the features of effective phonemic awareness instruction:

→ small-group or individual instruction

→ instruction that focused on at least two skills

→ instruction that lasted five to eighteen hours total (a more recent study suggests ten to twenty-four hours)

The more recent National Early Literacy Panel report (2008) focused on children from birth through age five and found that phonological awareness (e.g., rhyme, syllables, words, phonemes) predicted decoding as well. Because this analysis did not differentiate between phonemic awareness and insight about larger units of sound such as words, rhymes, or syllables, the panel conducted a secondary analysis. In that analysis, they found phoneme awareness to be a better predictor of decoding than rhyme awareness. This clarifies that the most important unit for children to understand is the *phoneme,* the individual speech sound, not rhyming.

Phonemic Awareness Instruction Paired with Letters Is More Effective Than Instruction Without Letters

Importantly, phonemic awareness instruction should not be oral only or uncombined with letters. Researchers compared phonemic awareness programs that used letters at some point in the instruction with those that did not (Ehri et al. 2001) to see if using letters improved spelling and reading. Phonemic awareness instruction that had letters *did* have a superior effect on spelling and reading when compared to instruction that did not use letters. The findings indicate that, at some point in a lesson, letters should be coordinated with phonemic awareness instruction.

With Coordinated Letter Instruction, About Twenty-Four Hours of Phonemic Awareness Instruction Is Beneficial

In 2024, researchers conducted a meta-analysis (a) to establish the optimal amount of cumulative instructional time that improved phonemic awareness performance and (b) to examine if adding letter instruction influenced that optimal amount of time (Erbeli et al. 2024). They examined sixteen studies with over six hundred students who were in preschool through grade 1. Once students had received 10.20 hours of oral-only phonemic awareness instruction (no letters), the maximum benefit was derived. However, if letters were also included, the optimal cumulative instructional time increased with benefits continuing through twenty-four hours of instruction. Researchers explained their results in this way: "Incorporating letters to PA instruction and PA into alphabetic instruction would be considered a practically meaningful and effective way to maximize PA gains. It is important to note that the curve's endpoint corresponds to the latest available dosage data point for this subset of studies, which was at twenty-four hours" (Erbeli et al. 2024, 20).

Young Children Can Detect Phonemes

Based on a previous study of the development of phonological awareness, the field has held that children develop awareness of larger sound units (e.g., rhyme, syllables) prior to smaller sound units (e.g., phonemes) and that children younger than four typically do not detect phonemes (Anthony et al. 2003). Curriculum designers have applied this principle by starting with tasks that included rhymes and syllables to build capacity for awareness of phonemes. A more recent study challenged this perspective (Kenner et al. 2017). Researchers noted that the types of measures supporting this "larger-to-smaller" developmental pattern were all "production tasks." In other words, the measures required children to produce sounds or perform tasks of tapping or moving counters to represent sounds. Instead, this team designed easier, receptive measures that only required children to point to correct answers using pictures.

The Kenner team specifically examined phonemic segmentation and blending in two- and three-year-old children. The measures presented children with pictures and the researchers pronounced a segmented or blended word corresponding with one of the pictures (e.g., "Point to the picture that shows /c/ /a/ /t/."). The findings showed that three-year-olds were able to identify the correct pictures for blended and segmented words at levels that were higher than chance. Blending sounds was easier than segmenting. The researchers wrote, "Overall, these findings indicate that contrary to prevailing wisdom, there are emerging phonemic awareness capacities prior to the age of four, and that these emerging abilities follow a predicted developmental progression of success when using more developmentally appropriate receptive phonemic awareness measures" (Kenner et al. 2017, 1589). Young children can and do have insights about individual speech sounds, or phonemes.

Phonemic Segmentation Enhances Decoding Skills

Several studies examined the phonological awareness skills of beginning readers to see if awareness of phonemes was more important to future word reading than awareness of larger sounds (e.g., rime—b-ag/t-ag) (Hulme et al. 2002; Muter et al. 1998; Nation and Hulme 1997). Researchers presented five-and-a-half-year-olds with tests that required them to demonstrate awareness of initial sounds, final consonants, onsets, and rimes. They used non-words. Each sound unit was also tested within three different tasks: (a) sound detection ("Choose the one that sounds like___."); (b) oddity tasks ("Which one doesn't belong?"); and (c) sound deletion ("Say *spag* without the /s/.").

After several months, the researchers tested children's word-reading accuracy to see which sound units best predicted word reading. Awareness of onset and rimes (e.g., b-at, d-og) was easier for children than awareness of initial and final sounds, but initial sound awareness predicted future word reading accuracy the best.

Importantly, the researchers did not interpret their findings to suggest that phonemic awareness training should focus *only* on phonemes. They wrote, "We do not believe that it would be optimal to concentrate exclusively on training phonemic skills in young children and those with early reading problems" (Hulme et al. 2002, 20). From our perspective, the findings suggest that if onset-rime or syllable instruction is not progressing, then teachers should move on to instruction on phonemes.

So What? Actions for the Classroom

Teach Phonemic Awareness in Short Sessions That Engage Children

In many respects, what we know about phonemic awareness instruction has not changed. The messages are simple: Do it! Make sure that children are paying attention and can receive feedback on their responses in small groups or individually. Activities should address multiple skills (e.g., saying sounds, finding a sound that doesn't belong, pointing to pictures that match a target sound, segmenting sounds at different levels such as words, syllables, onset-rime, and phonemes). Sessions should be engaging and active. They should help make sounds concrete by using pictures or hand motions or counters to represent sounds, and, of course, letters as well. On balance, instruction that lasts 10–24 hours in total, and no more, is what is needed. Translated into classroom practice, 10–24 hours might mean 60–144 sessions of 10 minutes each across a school year of 180 days. This ballpark figure must be interpreted alongside the age and literacy skills of the students. We could see kindergartners doing some form of phonemic awareness every day and first graders doing it about half that time. The quantity of phonemic awareness instruction should not be the only factor taken into consideration.

Teach Larger Units First, But Move to the Phoneme

There have been some new findings that indicate how best to teach phonemic awareness. The research evidence suggests that awareness of individual phonemes (e.g., /sh/ /i/ /p/) is what is most closely related to reading. This makes sense; the alphabet is a code for phonemes, individual speech sounds. When teaching young children, start with larger units, teaching words, syllables, and onsets and rimes, but then move to smaller units. The newest findings indicate that while starting with larger units is a good idea, mastery of those units is not necessary in order to introduce the most important unit, the phoneme. In other words, you do not need to hold off on working with phonemes until students have mastered larger units. If students are not mastering rhyme, for example, move on to phoneme-based skills such as identifying initial sounds or matching pictures that both start with the same beginning sounds. Rhyming is fun and worth doing but not as influential on future reading as phoneme awareness and should not be overemphasized.

To Support Letter-Sound Learning, Work on Initial Phoneme Activities

Phoneme-level skills are the most critical for learning, and within phoneme skills there are two levels that are closely related to phonics instruction. As children are learning letter sounds, pair instruction with activities that help them isolate, produce, and/or match the beginning sounds in words. For example, before, during, or after teaching the match between a letter (Tt) and sound (/t/), ask students to play oral alliterative games. For example, *Tommy Turtle likes* . . . (*tables, tea, teams, tails, tags, toast,* and so on). Picture sorts are also useful. Children identify pictures that match a target sound, sorting them from those that do not have the target sound. As the activities become more challenging, children should be producing the sounds themselves as opposed to the teacher doing it (e.g., "Tell me the sound you hear at the beginning of *toe*"). These kinds of activities will frontload or prime children's insights about beginning sounds.

Children can memorize responses without truly understanding a concept or having the insight that oral words are composed of phonemes. For example, a child could know to say the sound /t/ when the teacher points to the Tt, but when she tries to spell a word like *tape* has no insight that this word starts with the same sound. Make sure that the phonemic awareness instruction is coordinated with letter and phonics instruction. For example, do not do the phonemic awareness activities at a time that is separate from phonics instruction. Match the sounds from the phonics/letter instruction with those that are taking place during phonemic awareness. If letter-sound lessons have focused on Bb, Ss, Tt, Mm, and Vv, then use those sounds during phonemic awareness instruction.

To Support Decoding, Do Phonemic Segmentation and Blending Activities

The second important phonemic awareness skill, one that is highly related to sounding out or decoding, is fully segmenting and blending words orally (e.g., *gap* = /g/ /a/ /p/). This finding seems a bit counterintuitive, because decoding words *is* blending sounds together—but the act of orally segmenting, which is harder, does build capacity for decoding. So, do activities that break down the word fully into each sound using hand motions (e.g., chopping, tapping) or pushing counters into boxes (e.g., Elkonin boxes). Do this orally at first, with non-letter tokens or with hand motions, and then add letters. Phonemic segmentation and blending activities are a good warm-up right before decoding practice. For example, students might use Elkonin boxes to break up or segment words using tokens. Blending instruction goes the other way: the teacher provides sounds and students put them together (e.g., "What word do these sounds make? /t/-/a/-/p/?").

When segmenting and blending, start with words that have two phonemes and then move to those with three.

Integrate Oral Phonemic Awareness Actions (Motions, Tapping, Boxes) with Letters Promptly

Many of the studies that show the impact of phonemic awareness included activities that were oral and/or used non-letter manipulatives such as pictures, hand motions, or counters. However, these studies did not stop with the non-letter manipulatives. Right after doing an oral-only activity, children were asked to find letters or use letters. For example, a teacher might have students break up the sounds in *step* orally and then choose the letters to match the sounds.

Activities that focus on the phonemic skills without letters are honing in on the hardest part of the equation, the least intuitive part—the phonemes. Activities that go straight to letters may or may not be focusing on phonemic awareness (Kilpatrick 2015). Here is an example of teaching a phonemic skill and then adding letters: "We need to spell the word *tip*. Let's stretch it slowly. How many sounds do you hear? Yes! Three. Let's say them: /t/ /i/ /p/. Now let's write the first sound, /t/. I'll write the letter Tt." We can't imagine that you would do quality phonemic awareness without, at times, using concrete items or prompts that are not letters.

Phoneme Manipulation, Segmentation, and Deletion Develop Alongside Decoding Skills

You will notice that the research in this section does not address advanced phonemic awareness skills such as phoneme substitution or deletion (e.g., "What do you have when you take /p/ off of *pop*? (*–op*) What do you have when you change the /r/ in *ran* to /t/? (*tan*)"). These tasks do tend to appear in research studies and in comprehensive tests of phonemic awareness. But several studies suggest that these skills seem to require reading skills (Perfetti et al. 1987; Stahl and Murray 1994; Yopp 1992). Think about it. If you were asked this question, you would likely store the word visually in your mind (*ran*) and then visually replace the letters (*tan*) mentally. We could not find experimental research to support doing advanced phoneme deletion and substitution tasks to improve reading.

How should I teach phonological awareness (PA)?

Twenty-four Hours of *Total* Cumulative Instructional Time: PA with Letters

Twenty-four hours of instruction breaks down like this:

- 1,440 minutes
- 144 days with 10-minute lessons

Instruction should be engaging:

- Children should be **saying** their responses.

"The sounds in *bad*: /b/ /a/ /d/."

Focus on the PHONEME

- Young children can detect phonemes (Kenner et al. 2017).
- Phoneme awareness is a better predictor than rhyming (National Early Literacy Panel 2008).

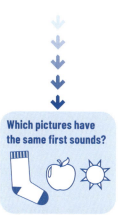

Which pictures have the same first sounds?

Incorporate Letters

- PA instruction that used letters *at some point* was more effective (Ehri et al. 2001).
- Use pictures, tokens, hand motions, and oral responses—but always add letters.
- Coordinate PA with phonics scope and sequence.

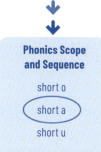

Phonics Scope and Sequence

short o
short a
short u

Phoneme Segmentation Builds Decoding

- Segmenting phonemes is more important to future word reading than onset-rime instruction (Hulme et al. 2002; Muter et al. 1998; Nation and Hulme 1997).

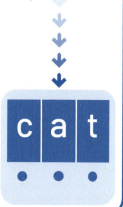

c a t

Other Useful Resources

Muter, V., C. Hulme, M. Snowling, and S. Taylor. 1998. "Segmentation, Not Rhyming, Predicts Early Progress in Learning to Read." *Journal of Experimental Child Psychology* 71 (1): 3–27.

Nation, K., and C. Hulme. 1997. "Phonemic Segmentation, Not Onset-Rime Segmentation, Predicts Early Reading and Spelling Skills." *Reading Research Quarterly* 32 (2): 154–167.

Question 5

What does the research say about sound walls and teaching mouth moves?

Discussion from the Classroom

Just as three-cueing anchor charts proliferated in the heyday of guided reading, sound walls have proliferated during this Science of Reading era. We go into classrooms all the time and see sound walls with pictures of mouths forming phonemes. What we  see less often is teachers *using* the posters. If not used, sound wall pictures will just fade into the island of misfit toys like so many other educational fads. So, we wondered, what do studies with beginning readers tell us about *how* to use pictures and how they *affect* students? Phonemes have not only acoustic properties that can be heard but also physiological properties that can be felt. Our teeth, tongue, lips, and larynx are all part of phoneme production. The body does different things when it makes the sound /m/ versus the sound /t/. Thus, it makes sense to teach early literacy learners not just the graphemes and how the phonemes sound but also how phonemes feel. After diving into the research, we found a few surprises.

Background and Assumptions

Teaching children mouth movements is not new and has been part of many programs for years, most notably Lindamood-Bell (Lindamood and Lindamood 1975). The approach includes several parts:

→ **Articulatory gestures** (e.g., mouth moves): These are the movements that our tongue, teeth, lips, and vocal cords make to produce a sound. For example, when we say /f/, our teeth touch our bottom lip, air is hissed through our mouth, and our vocal cords do not vibrate.

→ **Articulatory pictures:** These are static illustrations of the mouth showing the positions of the tongue, teeth, and lips as the phoneme is being made.

Using articulatory gestures and pictures is supported by the motor theory of speech perception (Liberman and Mattingly 1985). This theory suggests that understanding speech sounds involves not only hearing but also the processes for making sounds, including articulatory gestures, the motor commands our brains give to our vocal tracts, feedback, and categorization of sounds based on how they are made.

Research Studies That Inform the Question

Boyer, N., and L. C. Ehri. 2011. "Contribution of Phonemic Segmentation Instruction with Letters and Articulation Pictures to Word Reading and Spelling in Beginners." *Scientific Studies of Reading* 15 (5): 440–470.

Castiglioni-Spalten, M. L., and L. C. Ehri. 2003. "Phonemic Awareness Instruction: Contribution of Articulatory Segmentation to Novice Beginners' Reading and Spelling." *Scientific Studies of Reading* 7 (1): 25–52.

Roberts, T. A. 2005. "Articulation Accuracy and Vocabulary Size Contributions to Phonemic Awareness and Word Reading in English Language Learners." *Journal of Educational Psychology* 97 (4): 601–616.

Roberts, T. A., P. F. Vadasy, and E. A. Sanders. 2018. "Preschoolers' Alphabet Learning: Letter Name and Sound Instruction, Cognitive Processes, and English Proficiency." *Early Childhood Research Quarterly* 44: 257–274.

Research Findings

Articulatory Pictures and Mouth Moves Add Value to Strong Alphabet Instruction

Teaching students mouth moves through articulatory pictures appears to enhance alphabet instruction. Helping students learn how to make sounds and what their mouths are doing as they make a sound adds another layer to matching the visual letter form with the phoneme it represents. In an experimental study, four-year-olds were randomly assigned to three different groups that mixed different elements of letter instruction (Roberts, Vadasy, and Sanders 2018). Students learned eight different letters over forty sessions. The groups were as follows:

a. Paired Associated Learning (PAL)—pairing the letter and sound and repeating
b. PAL + Orthographic Learning (OL)—PAL and learning to spell the letter when given the sound
c. PAL + Articulatory Learning (AL)—PAL and learning how to make the sounds in the mouth

The AL component involved using pictures and mirrors and noticing the mouth moves. The PAL component was very specific, with easy, repetitive games ripe for classroom translation. Results were quite complex, but the PAL treatment worked the best for the total sample and for the multilingual learners (MLs). Secondary analysis, however, suggested that the articulatory instruction was particularly effective for MLs. The combined instruction resulted in greater growth on letter-naming and letter-sound measures.

Articulatory Pictures and Moves Impact Phonemic Skills and Future Word Reading

Many believe that the research on mouth moves supports letter-sound acquisition. However, several studies examined how teaching the kinesthetic elements of phonemes enhanced phonemic awareness, not letter-sound correspondences. In one study, researchers experimentally tested whether kindergartners could better segment phonemes if they were taught through articulatory pictures and gestures (Castiglioni-Spalten and Ehri 2003). The students could not read words, but they did know letter-sound correspondences and were able to create partial alphabetic spellings. Kindergartners were randomly assigned to three groups: (1) Mouth treatment: sequence articulatory pictures of sounds correctly; (2) Ear treatment: sequence blocks representing phonemes in the correct sequence; or (3) Control: no treatment. Letters were not used. Children sequenced either blocks for the phonemes or pictures showing how the mouth made the sound. There was no difference in results between the Mouth and Ear treatments. Using either blocks or articulatory pictures helped students segment phonemes better than the control group.

In another study, preschoolers who knew letter names but could not read were taught phonemic segmentation (Boyer and Ehri 2011). They were randomly assigned to three groups: (1) Letters plus articulatory pictures (LPA); (2) Letters only (LO); and (3) Control: no treatment. The LPA instruction was extensive, involving the following activities:

→ using mirrors to watch the mouth make a move
→ matching articulatory pictures with spoken phonemes
→ matching articulatory pictures with letters
→ ordering articulatory pictures in proper sequence (phonemic segmentation)

Both the LPA and LO groups did better than the control group on phonemic segmentation, spelling, word reading, and non-word repetition. The articulatory pictures (LPA) group *did* learn to read new words better than the letters-only group (LO). However, this LPA group had more instructional time, which may explain the better performance on learning new words.

> Many have miscited these two studies (Boyer and Ehri 2011; Castiglioni-Spalten and Ehri 2003), claiming that they support the use of articulatory pictures for *letter learning*. In fact, these studies focused on *segmenting phonemes* (e.g., *big* =/b/ /i/ /g/), not on learning letters. The studies did not find that pictures or mouth moves helped with letters. It may be that looking at pictures and using them to segment adds a complex step to the task that is unnecessary for the average learner. The direct relationship with respect to alphabet learning and decoding is between the grapheme and phoneme. In both studies, the articulatory pictures and mouth moves resulted in better word learning.

In another study, researchers investigated the natural variation in reading skills of dual-language kindergarten and first graders (Hmong, Spanish) (Roberts 2005). The study collected data on students' abilities in English in (a) correctly articulating words; (b) vocabulary; (c) phonemic awareness; (d) letter-sound correspondences; and (e) word reading. For kindergartners, articulation predicted phonemic awareness, and for first graders, articulation predicted word reading.

Essentially, using articulatory pictures and mouth moves did not impact letter skills, but in one study influenced new word reading. Learning articulatory moves enhanced the phonemic awareness of multilingual kindergartners and the word reading skills of multilingual first graders.

So What? Actions for the Classroom

Use Articulatory Pictures and Mouth Moves Along with Other Instructional Features

In the rush to fill the walls with posters, educators should remember that many of the studies tested mouth moves along with other instructional features. These included the following:

→ letter cards: naming letters, naming sounds (e.g., Bb = "Bee" =/b/)

- visually discriminating between letters (e.g., t vs. f vs. i)
- using letters to "spell" sounds (e.g., write the letter for the sound you hear in *sat*)
- matching letters to pictures with the same first sound (e.g., put the letter Jj with pictures that start with /j/)
- using letters to phonemically segment words. (e.g., *"let"* = l-e-t)

To be readers, young children need to be able to acquire and use grapheme-phoneme relationships. The articulatory pictures serve that purpose; they are a means to the end of decoding. In several studies, the articulatory elements were not better than blocks or letters.

Use Articulatory Moves to Help Multilingual Learners

Two studies suggested that dual-language learners, particularly, benefited from articulatory pictures and learning mouth moves (Roberts 2005; Roberts, Vadasy, and Sanders 2018). Researchers explained it this way: "These results suggest that the instruction including attention to letter writing and articulation may have been more beneficial to dual-language learners than other children" (Roberts 2021, 13).

Once, in a school in Maryland, a teacher grabbed Heidi Anne in the hall and asked her to work with one of her multilingual learners. "I don't know what is going on. She knows the consonants but not the vowels." Heidi Anne sat down with the little girl, and after a little review, realized that she had not differentiated the vowel sounds. They all were a kind of flat schwa sound. With just a little bit of work showing her the differences between how the mouth makes short a, e, i, o, and u sounds, she got it!

Here is another explanation: Children whose native language is not English may not have heard certain English phonemes during their toddler years and may not use those phonemes in their homes. For example, the /j/ is not used in Spanish. Thus, multilingual learners may not be sensitive to hearing and/or producing certain sounds. When dual-language learners are taught extra information about phoneme articulation, they may develop awareness of phonemes both auditorily and physiologically in ways that help them apply it to sound-spellings and reading words. Mouth moves may give dual-language learners an extra boost.

Add Mouth Moves to Strong Phonics Instruction

Focus mostly on teaching students to say the phoneme associated with the letter. That is the target content. Show children how to make the sound with their mouths using articulatory gestures and pictures, but do not turn the focus toward identifying the pictures that match phonemes and graphemes. We are not teaching students to read lips, and many sounds actually look the same in a picture (e.g., f/v, s/z, p/b, t/d/, k/g).

Tell Students to DO IT!

Imagine that you are teaching someone to shoot a layup in basketball. Although pictures illustrating the steps are helpful at first, shooting layups is physical. It is best learned by doing and getting corrective feedback. Phonemes are speech sounds that are physical as well as auditory. What will really help students is not staring at pictures but actually moving their mouths and paying attention to how their mouths are working. So, it's all about *doing* it, not looking at static pictures. Several studies even have children use mirrors to watch their own mouths, and this can be very motivating. Mirror use also might help students naturally self-correct if they are saying a sound wrong.

What does the research say about teaching mouth moves?

Add mouth moves to strong phonics instruction.
- Emphasize graphemes and phonemes and then *add* articulatory gestures. The main content is the *letter* and *sound*. We are not teaching lip reading.

DO the moves. Use mirrors.
- Anchor charts are a back-up. Have students use mirrors to see their mouths. Tell them, "Watch my mouth."

Mouth moves are helpful with dual language learners.
- DLs may not come to school with knowledge of all the English phonemes. Teaching them mouth moves helps.

(Castiglioni-Spalten and Ehri 2003; Roberts 2005; Boyer and Ehri 2011; Roberts, Vadasy, and Sanders 2018)

Other Useful Resources

Liberman, A. M., and I. G. Mattingly. 1985. "The Motor Theory of Speech Perception Revised." *Cognition* 21 (1): 1–36.

Question 6

What does the research say about how decodable texts impact readers? How should I use decodable texts?

Discussion from the Classroom

Decodable texts tend to evoke strong opinions. On the one hand are teachers like Stella: "I can't stand them! Fat cats on mats! No way! The stories in these books are just not meaningful!" On the other hand are teachers like David: "If you are teaching kids how to read, decodables are essential! Why teach kids to sound out words and then give them a book with a word like *hair* that they can't sound out?" This recycled debate is as old as the more phonics/less phonics discussion that the field has every ten to twenty years. The pendulum swings back and forth between a heavy or light emphasis on decoding, and teachers get caught in the crossfire. What does the research say about decodability?

Background and Assumptions

→ **Decodable text:** To support beginning readers when they have incomplete knowledge of the patterns in English, decodable texts control the complexity of the words in books so that children can sound out the words. So, if a child has been taught certain grapheme-phoneme correspondences (GPCs) (e.g., single consonants, short a, e, o) and high-frequency words (e.g., *the, be, he, be, to, of, a, and, is*), then those words would appear in text (e.g., *The dog is hot. He is red.*). The coordination of phonics instruction with text decodability is often called *lesson-to-text-match*. Some define decodability based on phonetic regularity or consistency—one-to-one letter-sound relationships (e.g., *it, bag, pin*) (Saha et al. 2021).

- **High-frequency words:** Highly decodable texts also systematically include some of most frequently occurring words in English, even if the exact GPCs have not been explicitly taught (e.g., /th/ in *the*, /oo/ in *to*). You cannot read sentences in English without a handful of high-frequency words.

- **Decodability:** Instead of thinking about books as either decodable or not decodable, we believe that teachers should think about books on a continuum from highly decodable, with many words that the student knows or could decode, to least decodable, with very few, if any, words that the reader might be able to decode.

Least Decodable → **Most Decodable**

| Very few words that contain known patterns. | Few words contain known patterns. | Some words contain known patterns. Some words do not. | A lot of words contain known patterns. | Most words contain known patterns. |

Research Studies That Inform the Question

Cheatham, J. P., and J. H. Allor. 2012. "The Influence of Decodability in Early Reading Text on Reading Achievement: A Review of the Evidence." *Reading and Writing* 25 (9): 2223-2246.

Jenkins, J. R., J. A. Peyton, E. A. Sanders, and P. F. Vadasy. 2004. "Effects of Reading Decodable Texts in Supplemental First-Grade Tutoring." *Scientific Studies of Reading* 8 (1): 53–85.

Juel, C., and D. Roper. 1985. "The Influence of Basal Readers on First Grade Reading." *Reading Research Quarterly* 20 (2): 134–152.

Pugh, A., D. M. Kearns, and E. H. Hiebert. 2023. "Text Types and Their Relation to Efficacy in Beginning Reading Interventions." *Reading Research Quarterly* 58 (4): 710–732.

Saha, N. M., L. E. Cutting, S. Del Tufo, and S. Bailey. 2021. "Initial Validation of a Measure of Decoding Difficulty as a Unique Predictor of Miscues and Passage Reading Fluency." *Reading and Writing* 34 (2): 497–527.

Vadasy, P. F., and E. A. Sanders. 2009. "Supplemental Fluency Intervention and Determinants of Reading Outcomes." *Scientific Studies of Reading* 13 (5): 383–425.

Research Findings

Word Decodability and Frequency Influence Accurate Word Reading

Teachers have long assumed that students read regular, more decodable words (e.g., *hit, nap, pin*) more easily than less-regular, more complex words (e.g., *light, claw, hair*). In fact, research supports this assumption (Saha et al. 2021; Vadasy and Sanders 2009).

Researchers defined decodability using phonetic regularity or consistency as explained in the Background and Assumptions section above (Saha et al. 2021). They calculated a ratio between the number of phonemes in a word and the number of letters. For example, *cat* has three phonemes to three letters, or a ratio of 3:3, and is considered simple. In contrast, the word *eight* has two phonemes to five letters, or a ratio of 2:5, and is harder. The researchers found that the phonetic regularity and frequency of words predicted students' oral reading fluency and word errors during passage reading. Words that were more regular and/or more frequent were easier for students to read.

A similar study examined the fluency of struggling second and third graders based on word complexity (Vadasy and Sanders 2009). These researchers scored all words read in all texts on a nine-point scale of complexity. Students were less fluent and comprehended less in books that had more complex words, which included (a) single-syllable words with l- or r-controlled sounds—*fall, tore, cold*; (b) two-syllable inflected words with simple vowel patterns—*napping, biked*; and (c) single-syllable and two-syllable words with highly irregular patterns—*buy, earn, dinosaur, communication*.

Reading Highly Decodable Text Facilitates Accuracy

A literature review consolidated and reported the findings that explicitly studied the effects of text decodability on readers (Cheatham and Allor 2012). This was not a meta-analysis. Instead, researchers simply summarized the findings across seven studies (four descriptive studies and three experimental or quasi-experimental studies). Most studies paired systematic, explicit phonics instruction with decodable texts, and in many cases there was a match between the phonics instruction and the words in the books (Cheatham and Allor 2012). Students who read more highly decodable text applied a decoding (sounding out) word-reading strategy and students were more accurate in decodable materials. The review is useful, but the number of studies limits the application.

In First Grade, Highly Decodable Text Facilitates Decoding Skills and New Word Reading

Although older, a 1985 study was one of the few that tested the impact of decodable texts on entire classrooms of students as opposed to one-on-one or small-group instructional contexts. In this study, all students received the same scripted phonics instruction but read either (a) a basal reader that was decodable or (b) one that was based on a repetition of high-frequency words, like the old Dick and Jane series (Juel and Roper/Schneider 1985).

Students were tested three times—at the beginning, middle, and end of the year—and those using the decodable basal were better at decoding at the beginning and middle of the year. The children reading the decodable basal were better able to decode new, unknown words that they had never seen before at the end of the year. The findings suggested that, given the same phonics instruction, students who read a heavy diet of decodable texts tend to have superior skills in reading new, unknown words and a stronger decoding strategy through the first two-thirds of the year.

Within the Context of Interventions or One-on-One Tutoring, Decodable Text Is Not Highly Influential

The research suggests that in situations with focused one-one-one tutoring or targeted interventions, decodable text is not influential. A study of one-on-one tutoring provided the same phonics instruction to all participants and randomly assigned students to read more or less decodable texts (Jenkins et al. 2004). Students who received the more decodable text did no better than those who had less decodable text.

In a recent meta-analysis, researchers examined 120 intervention studies designed to help readers who were experiencing challenges (Pugh, Kearns, and Hiebert 2023). For each study, they identified whether the intervention used text and then what types of text (decodable vs. non-decodable). The analysis first examined if reading texts at all of any kind mattered. One hundred and six interventions asked students to read texts and fourteen others did not. Results did not differ in interventions that used text versus those that did not. The second analysis examined if student performance differed in the studies that used decodable text versus those that used non-decodable text. There were no differences in student performance between decodable and non-decodable texts. Interventions using decodable texts did not result in students who were more successful than those that did not.

However, in eight studies, seven of which used one-on-one tutoring, student performance was better in interventions using both decodable and non-decodable texts (Pugh, Kearns, and Hiebert 2023). In other words, with a tutor, students benefited from instruction using both text types. How did instructors use these two types? In some studies, students read both highly decodable and less decodable texts at the same time. In another study, students first read highly decodable texts for a period of ten weeks and then read other vocabulary-controlled texts. In another study, students read decodables in the first grade and then trade books in the second grade.

These studies suggest that in a carefully specified intervention, explicit, systematic phonics instruction with a skilled teacher is more powerful than text. This is particularly true if the setting is a one-on-one format.

So What? Actions for the Classroom

Coordinate Highly Decodable Text with a Phonics Scope and Sequence

In all the studies, decodable texts were used alongside explicit, systematic phonics instruction. In fact, some studies defined highly decodable text based on the lesson-to-text match. This means that you must be following a scope and sequence and teaching explicitly for students to benefit from highly decodable texts. You cannot simply plop a book in front of a student and expect that student to decode the words just because the book is called "decodable." Books don't teach students letter sounds or how to blend words, teachers do. When choosing decodable texts, note that they should list the focal patterns and high-frequency words they target on the back cover or at the front or back of the book (e.g., short a: *bag, tan, hat, nag, cap*; high-frequency words: *the, to, is*). Texts with decodability are only readable to students if they have the skills to decode the patterns in the book.

Ensure That Students Are "Decodable Ready"

The research suggests that highly decodable texts enhance accuracy and fluency. However, you will not get those benefits if students do not have the prerequisites in place. What kind of skills do researchers make sure students have *before* asking them to read a decodable text? Those skills appear to be (a) automatic recognition of letter sounds; (b) print tracking; (c) recognition of some high-frequency words; and (d) the ability to blend or sound out a word on their own.

Think about it—at the end of first grade, students should be able to read fifty words per minute. If each word has three or four letters, that's 150 to 200 letters that must be processed in under a minute. When you decode, you can't stop and pause and think about the letter sound. Also, students should be able to find the beginning of a word and track print. Lastly, students need a lot of practice blending sounds together in individual words before you give them a book with fifty or more words. To get the benefit of the decodable book, students need to do some practice first.

Use Highly Decodable Texts in the Early Stages of Literacy (mid-K to mid-first-grade)

Many of the studies on highly decodable texts take place at the beginning stages of literacy, which is typically mid-kindergarten to mid-first-grade. This is the point at which students have the tools to start to sound out words, but they do not know all the vowel patterns in English. Highly decodable texts are like training wheels. Eventually, everything becomes decodable because readers have acquired the major graphemes in English and the training wheels can come off. In fact, as students learn the major graphemes and progress, more and more patterns are readable and there is less need to manipulate text decodability.

If you give a student a book with too many patterns, all they can do is use beginning sounds and guess. A highly decodable book will jumpstart their application of phonics knowledge. In one paper, theorists suggested that readers might benefit from highly decodable texts as they transition from the partial alphabetic phase of word reading, when they use only beginning and ending letters, to the full alphabetic phase, when they can fully decode all sounds, including the medial vowel sound. We agree.

Use Highly Decodable Texts When Students Do Not Have a Knowledgeable Teacher by Their Side

The intervention research suggests that when students have phonics instruction and the benefit of one-on-one tutoring, highly decodable text is not very influential (Jenkins et al. 2004; Pugh, Kearns, and Hiebert 2023). When using less-decodable text, a ready adult can provide the appropriate prompts to support decoding and accuracy. Conversely, when a student is going to need to read independently or take a book home, then the match between their phonics and high-frequency word knowledge may be more critical.

Hold Students Accountable for Highly Decodable Text

In all of the studies we reviewed, students were expected to read highly decodable text on their own. This might sound like an odd statement, but there have been many approaches to beginning reading in which teachers actually "pre-read" texts to students. This means that teachers read the book before they ask students to do it. If you have to read the book for the student, then it is not a book that *the student* can read. When it comes to highly decodable text, if you pre-read, you are actually throwing out the entire purpose of giving students practice applying their phonics knowledge in a connected text.

Cautions and Caveats

→ Avoid overvaluing or undervaluing highly decodable texts. They are tools that teachers can use when students are beginning readers. As students learn more and more vowel patterns, everything becomes decodable naturally.

→ Highly decodable texts can contain odd words that are not in students' vocabularies. Decoding any word must lead to recognizing it as a word the reader knows. So, if you come to a word like *jig*, make sure that readers know what that is. And avoid books that have too many words that are not in students' vocabularies.

→ Specifying the exact contribution of decodabilty is challenging. In many studies, text decodabilty is combined with other instructional variables, such a vowel flexing, mispronunciation correction (Savage et al. 2018), one-on-one tutoring (Jenkins et al. 2004), or other text types that are used across classroom and intervention contexts (Jenkins et al. 2004; Pugh, Kearns, and Hiebert 2023).

What does the research say about decodable texts?

- More frequent words are easier to read. (e.g., *the*, *to*, *and*, *for*).

- Decodable words are easier to read. They include taught letter-sounds or transparent patterns (e.g., b-a-g = bag).

- Readers are more accurate with decodable text.

- Readers experiencing difficulty are less fluent and comprehend less in texts with words that are less decodable (e.g., *fall*, *tore*, *napped*, *biking*, *buy*, *earn*, *dinosaur*).

- Within the context of one-on-one tutoring, decodable text is not highly influential.

(Justice et al. 2009; Nevo and Vaknin-Nusbaum 2018; Farry-Thorn and Treiman 2022)

Other Useful Resources

Foorman, B. R., D. J. Francis, K. C. Davidson, M. W. Harm, and J. Griffin. 2004. "Variability in Text Features in Six Grade 1 Basal Reading Programs." *Scientific Studies of Reading* 8 (2): 167–197.

Question 7

How many times does a reader need to decode a word in order to really learn it?

Discussion from the Classroom

Recently, there has been a great deal of discussion about orthographic mapping and its importance in helping students store words cognitively for later retrieval. We see more emphasis on teaching children how to blend sounds together in words. We see discouragement of asking students to memorize high-frequency words. We see books set up to provide multiple opportunities to decode taught patterns. We have seen more emphasis on cumulative practice and review.

With all this emphasis on mapping words, however, we have bumped into a very common question, articulated by Emma, an award-winning reading specialist: "How many times exactly do readers need to encounter a word in order to map it into memory?" Such a great question! But the research suggests that the answer depends on several things:

- → the reader's skill
- → the type of word being decoded (e.g., consistent—*cat* vs. different ways to spell the same sound —long o: *hope, boat, tow*)
- → the context in which the word is being read (e.g., word presented alone vs. in text)

So, based on the research, there are slightly different answers for different readers, words, and contexts.

Background and Assumptions

The research focusing on the number of reading exposures heavily emphasizes several models, one called *orthographic mapping* and the other called *self-teaching*. In many studies, researchers use *pseudowords* to test mapping skills.

→ **Orthographic mapping:** In the simplest of terms, orthographic mapping is readers connecting the visual system of written letters and larger spelling patterns to spoken systems, including phonemes (e.g., *dig* =/d/ /i/ /g/), syllables (e.g., ta-ble), and morphemes (e.g., in-cred-ible). Ultimately, mapping also connects words to a reader's stored knowledge of meaning, a mental lexicon.

  Orthographic mapping creates connections between spelling patterns and sounds, leading to readers storing words by sight and retrieving them instantaneously. Orthographic mapping does not rely on any cues unrelated to sound-spelling relationships, including the visual shape of a word, letter sequences unconnected to sound units (e.g., knowing *look* has two o's without knowing the sound), word length, or contextual guessing (e.g., using pictures) (Ehri 2014).

→ **Self-teaching:** The self-teaching hypothesis is *not* about children teaching themselves. Instead, it is a model that hypothesizes that as readers learn the alphabetic code to associate written words with their spoken words, they can use that knowledge to decode new, unknown words (Share 1995).

  The self-teaching hypothesis has two parts: (1) that letter-sound knowledge gives a reader the mechanism to translate words into oral pronunciations and (2) that the knowledge of letter sounds provides opportunities for readers to independently decode new, never-before-seen words, ones that are "self-taught." For example, if readers encounter a word like *dab* and know the letter-sound patterns, they can decode that word. Self-teaching is ignited by explicit, systematic phonics and morphology instruction that provides the reader with enough information to decode new, unknown words. Share (1995) called phonological decoding and self-teaching the "sine qua non" of reading acquisition. The Latin phrase means "without which not"—without decoding skill and self-teaching, literacy acquisition cannot go forward.

→ **Pseudowords:** These are made-up words that follow legal spelling patterns in a language (e.g., *vait, tem, shrusk*). They are used by researchers to study how students learn new words because if experimenters use real words, they cannot know if the learning is attributed to students' previous knowledge of the words or the variables in their studies.

Research Studies That Inform the Question

Nation, K., P. Angell, and A. Castles. 2007. "Orthographic Learning via Self-Teaching in Children Learning to Read English: Effects of Exposure, Durability, and Context." *Journal of Experimental Child Psychology* 96 (1): 71–84.

Reitsma, P. 1983. "Printed Word Learning in Beginning Readers." *Journal of Experimental Child Psychology* 36 (2): 321–339.

Research Findings ⬅⬅⬅⬅⬅

Depending on the Regularity of the Word, Readers Took Between Three and Six Exposures to Learn It

In a study conducted with Dutch children, three experiments directly answer questions about (a) how many times readers needed to see patterns before knowing them; (b) the impact of regular versus less-regular letter patterns (regular sounds are mostly spelled one way, e.g. *hit* and *bag*, while less-regular sounds can be spelled more than one way, e.g., the long o in *soap, hope,* and *tow*); and (c) the impact of a reader's skills on the number of trials needed (Reitsma 1983).

Note: Both English and Dutch have "semi-transparent" spelling systems, which means they contain patterns that are less regular. In these languages, (a) two or more letters can represent some speech sounds (e.g., *th, ch, eight*); (b) there is more than one way to spell some speech sounds (e.g., long e: ea/ee/ey *meat, greet, key*); and (c) some letters represent more than one sound (e.g., c/s).

In the study's first experiment, researchers examined how quickly third graders could learn regular, consistent words. To ensure that the participants had not seen the words before, the researchers used pseudowords, words that are not real but conform with patterns that are used in Dutch. The readers learned to match regular, unknown words to pictures (e.g., *plom* = picture of a dish). They also matched real words to pictures as a point of comparison (e.g., *apple* = picture of an apple). With the unknown words, there were two conditions: (1) seeing the spelling and hearing the word orally or (2) just hearing the word orally. After learning the unknown words, readers were tested on their accuracy and speed matching words to pictures. The study showed that students learned the regular, unknown words better when they saw the spellings and heard the pronunciations. With *regular* words (e.g., *mat, tip, red*), experienced third graders learned words with three practice trials.

In the second and third experiments, researchers investigated how quickly first graders learned word-specific, less-regular patterns in unknown words (e.g., long o—*hope*, *boat*, *tow*). They also investigated the number of times it took to map a word and if this differed by reader skill. Several days after learning the words, students were asked to read them with researchers measuring the accuracy and time to decode the words. In the second experiment, first graders who had eight exposures read the words with the most accuracy and the most quickly. In the third experiment, readers at different skill levels (the study terms were *skilled*, *less skilled*, and *learning disabled*) learned words in different conditions, with readers getting two, four, or six practice exposures. The learning-disabled students read the words more accurately and quickly with six exposures.

→ With less-regular words (e.g., *soap, hope, tow*), both typically developing and learning-disabled first graders retained words better after six practice trials.

A different experiment examined how self-teaching worked in typically developing English-speaking second and third graders (Nation, Angell, and Castles 2007). The study examined (a) the impact of the number of exposures on word learning and (b) the retention of learning after one and seven days.

Less-regular pseudowords (e.g., *ferd, meem*) were used in this study. Because self-teaching was the study's objective, students were not trained to read the words. Instead, readers were presented with the words once, twice, or four times. After one and seven days, students were tested on their abilities to identify the correct target words (e.g., *ferd*) when the targets were mixed with three similar words (e.g., *furd, ferp, furp*). The number of words that students accurately identified was the outcome variable in the study. The results showed the following:

→ Average second and third graders "self-taught" the most unknown words with four exposures as compared to one (60 percent vs. 43 percent).

Words in Context Are Not Mapped Faster Than Words in Isolation

The study also examined the impact of presenting words in context rather than isolated (Nation, Angell, and Castles 2007). Earlier theoretical work suggested that context plays some role in self-teaching, so in the experiment described above, half of the students were presented words that were embedded into stories and half were presented with words in isolated card piles. Words presented within the context of stories were not self-taught better than the ones that were presented in isolation. This suggests that reading words within the context of a story does not lead to better orthographic mapping. Contextual word reading does not advance self-teaching more than reading words in isolation nor does it hurt self-teaching. They both facilitate self-teaching equally as long as the reader is actually decoding.

So What? Actions for the Classroom

Focus First on Letter-Sound Patterns in Systematic, Explicit Phonics

Although the question in this section is about how many times students need to be exposed to words, that question misses the foundation of word learning—how students retain words. Teachers should not be thinking about the number of times they present a specific word, per se, but the degree to which a student possesses the letter sounds to decode it. Then, perhaps, the number of exposures should be considered. Word learning requires systematic phonics and morphological instruction using a scope and sequence and explicit instructional talk that connects visual symbols and sounds. Once students have some fluency in blending words using their knowledge, they can self-teach and read many words they have never seen before. The trick is knowing how to spell them, which spellings go with which sounds (e.g., *grate* vs. *grait*). So it's the system and not the repetitions of individual items or words that we focus on.

This is important because we could not possibly create instruction in which we expose children to all the words that they will need to be skilled readers, nor should we. Children will encounter words in text that we have not taught them. That's like giving them a "fish for a day." Instead, we want to *teach them how to fish,* to recognize unknown words because they know the system. Phonological decoding and knowledge of patterns is what will ignite self-teaching. It does not matter if you present a word three, five, or twenty times if the students do not know the letter sounds upon which the word is built. (See below for an exception with word-specific, variable spellings.)

Adjust the Number of Practice Times Based on the Regularity of the Word and the Skills of the Readers

The research findings point to the fact that different types of words and readers will require different levels of practice. For regular words and for more skilled readers, less repetition may be needed. If the word is a regular word with a consistent spelling, such as *chip, fish, trap,* or *bag,* then students don't need to practice the word as much. In the study, they only needed to practice these words three times (Reitsma 1983). Once students learn the pattern, they can use it across words. When first graders or other less-experienced readers are learning a pattern for the first time, the number might be more than three.

With words that have variable spellings (e.g., *hate, paint, day, eight*), students need more practice. In first grade, students needed at least six exposures to learn word-specific patterns (e.g., *oa = soap, o_e = hope*). Younger readers with learning disabilities also did better with up to six exposures with words like this. Words with variable spellings are more challenging because the same sound can be spelled different ways. Students must learn word-specific patterns. The only way to know that *soap* is *oa* and *hope* is *o_e* is to see those words repeatedly.

If the Word Has Sounds That Could be Spelled in Multiple Ways, Go for More Practice Times

In this series of experiments across different grades, different types of words, and different skill levels, words that were presented six times were learned better than words than words that were presented fewer times. Although not precise, the trend suggests that if a teacher does not have a great deal of information about the reader or is not thinking about the pattern, a goal of six presentations might be a good ballpark. This level of repetition was also found in a study of at-risk first graders learning high-frequency words (Steacy et al. 2020).

Ignite Self-Teaching by Supporting Application of Phonics Knowledge, but Also Review New Words

With all the talk of explicit phonics instruction and trying to pin down the details, like how many times a word should be presented, we can forget that the very point of phonics is that it is a self-sustaining system. In the second study, researchers established that skilled readers can self-teach new words in different conditions. They can decode unfamiliar words whether they are presented in isolation or found in stories. This means they don't use context to self-teach. Therefore, as students learn patterns and encounter new words, we can expect them to decode the words and to apply their knowledge. However, the findings also suggest that we should follow up after students encounter a new word, because successful self-teaching only occurred for 60 percent of the words (at the most). If a student is unable to decode 40 percent of the new words in a text, we would not say that was acceptable. Our suggestion: If the student knows a pattern in a new word, let them try to decode it without you. See what they can do. But circle back to see if they decoded correctly.

Cautions and Caveats

→ There are reasons to question this question about the number of times to present specific words. If the way that we coded speech into print had no system, then we would need to memorize each word, and the number of times we encountered words would be highly impactful. We would have nothing to help remember which symbols went with which words.

However, English (along with many other languages) is alphabetic; there is a system. Visual symbols and combinations of those symbols represent speech sounds. That is why readers can pronounce pseudowords that they have never seen before (e.g., *lig, peight*). The difficulty comes if there is more than one way to spell a sound (e.g., *peight, pate, pait*). As the research bears out, repetitions of words are most important in those situations. In those cases, readers benefit from more encounters. With patterns that are very consistent, such as the closed-syllable pattern (cvc, cvcc, ccvc), once you have the system, you can read any word that has that pattern.

→ Lab studies like the ones described here do not directly generalize to classroom practice. The findings involve pseudowords and short-term interventions. The number of exposures in these studies points to patterns or trends as opposed to absolute dictates.

→ These studies did not analyze words with multiple syllables, and for this reason, we cannot draw any conclusions about how many times multisyllabic words need to be repeated.

How many times does a reader need to decode a word to learn it? It depends on the **reader** and the **word**.

Is the reader a beginner?
→ More repetitions are needed.

Is the reader experiencing reading difficulties?
→ More repetitions are needed.

Does the reader know the code?
They can apply it to words they have seen zero times, even "pseudo" words (*pleightly, vafting*).

Words in context are *not* orthographically mapped better than words in isolation.

Is the GPC in the word highly consistent?
Is it pronounced the same way across most words?

play coat boy dig hat ship

→ Fewer repetitions are needed, possibly one or none.

Is the GPC in the word variable?
Can it be pronounced more than one way (e.g., ea, ow, oo)?

meat great head bow how book tool

→ More repetitions are needed.

(Nation, Angell, and Castles 2007; Reitsma 1983)

Other Useful Resources

Ehri, L. C. 2014. "Orthographic Mapping in the Acquisition of Sight Word Reading, Spelling Memory, and Vocabulary Learning." *Scientific Studies of Reading* 18 (1): 5–21.

Steacy, L. M., D. Fuchs, J. K. Gilbert, D. M. Kearns, A. M. Elleman, and A. A. Edwards. 2020. "Sight Word Acquisition in First Grade Students at Risk for Reading Disabilities: An Item-Level Exploration of the Number of Exposures Required for Mastery." *Annals of Dyslexia* 70 (2): 259–274.

Question 8

How should I teach high-frequency sight words? Should students just memorize them visually?

Discussion from the Classroom

Sight-word mania! That's what we call it when a school goes wild with sight words. It usually happens something like this: Part of the K–3 literacy assessment includes lists of high-frequency words, words that show up a lot in books that children will need to read. Teachers assess these words at the beginning, middle, and end of the year, along with other phonics skills. Then, someone gets the idea that teaching sight words is low-hanging fruit and an easy way to increase performance on the literacy assessment. Suddenly, sight words are everywhere. Sight words on cards! Sight words on lists going home! Sight words in the reading resource room! Sight words with the volunteer! Sight words on smartboards! Sight words in preK! And it's all about just looking at those sight words and visually memorizing them or maybe just noting the first sound. And kids do learn the sight words, at least enough of them to make the literacy assessments at midyear and the end of the year look better. Students even seem to be reading their first grade books better. It's a hit! Sight-word mania works . . . until it doesn't.

For most readers between second and third grade, visually memorizing whole words breaks down. Suddenly, using partial cues like the two o's in *look* doesn't work anymore. There are too many words, and the system of organizing words is unreliable and unstructured. Yet high-frequency words *do* have irregular patterns. Do you teach someone to sound out *the*, *said*, or *of*? What if they don't know the *th* digraph? How should you teach high-frequency words?

Background and Assumptions

→ **High-frequency word:** A high-frequency word is one that appears a great deal in English (e.g., *the*, *to*, *he*, and *I*). Linguists and educators have developed lists of high-frequency words based on collections of words in large samples (e.g., Fry 1980; Dolch 1936). Many high-frequency words are "function" words, in that they do not convey the main meaning of the sentence but are still needed to create syntactically correct sentences (e.g., prepositions, articles, auxiliary verbs, pronouns). Some high-frequency words have spellings that are less regular, such as *the*, *is*, *to*, or *for*.

→ **Irregular/less-regular words:** English is a deep orthography, which means that, although letters represent speech sounds, there are some words that do not follow typical patterns (e.g., *was*, *done*). Actually, "regularity lies on a continuum from completely regular words (e.g., *dog*), to words with only one irregular grapheme-phoneme correspondence (e.g., *find*), to highly irregular words with many irregular correspondences (e.g., *aisle*, *meringue*)" (Colenbrander et al. 2020, 97).

→ **Sight words:** Occasionally, people will use the term *sight word* incorrectly to refer to high-frequency words. They believe children should be taught to visually memorize high-frequency words by sight because some high-frequency words have irregularities (e.g., *to*, *of*, *said*). In fact, all words, irregular and regular, can eventually become sight words, automatically recognized. So, the terms *sight word* and *high-frequency word* are not interchangeable.

→ **Set for variability, mispronunciation correction, and SPAAR:** Mispronunciation correction is a strategy used to ask readers to cross-check a mispronounced word against words they know. Often, mispronunciation occurs when readers partially decode highly irregular words using a regularized pronunciation, such as decoding the word *yacht* as /yatched/ (Elbro et al. 2012; Hilte and Reitsma 2006). If readers have a "set for variability," a broad base of vocabulary against which they can check a decoded word, then they can make corrections, such as, "No, not /yatched/. That's not a word. It's /yaucht/ like the boat." In one study, this is called "Semantic and Phonological Ability to Adjust Recoding," or SPAAR (Kearns et al. 2016).

Research Studies That Inform the Question

Colenbrander, D., H. C. Wang, T. Arrow, and A. Castles. 2020. "Teaching Irregular Words: What We Know, What We Don't Know, and Where We Can Go from Here." *The Educational and Developmental Psychologist* 37 (2): 97–104.

Ehri, L. C. 2005. "Learning to Read Words: Theory, Findings, and Issues." *Scientific Studies of Reading* 9 (2): 167–188.

Steacy, L. M., D. Fuchs, J. K. Gilbert, D. M. Kearns, A. M. Elleman, and A. A. Edwards. 2020. "Sight Word Acquisition in First Grade Students at Risk for Reading Disabilities: An Item-Level Exploration of the Number of Exposures Required for Mastery." *Annals of Dyslexia* 70 (2): 259–274.

Research Findings ⬅ ⬅ ⬅ ⬅

Readers' Decoding, Spelling, and Vocabulary Skills Helped Them Learn Less-Regular Words

Because some high-frequency words are less regular, research on learning less-regular words informs the teaching of high-frequency words. One study examined fifth graders' reading of irregular words (e.g., *give*, *have*) (Steacy et al. 2020). Researchers examined features of words and the skills of students that affected word reading. They also looked at how student disability influenced their ability to read irregular words, investigating differences between early reading-disabled students (ERD), late reading-disabled students (LRD), and typically developing readers (TD). Findings showed that students' (a) decoding skills; (b) knowledge of correct spellings (e.g., *rain* or *rane*); and (c) vocabulary knowledge influenced their abilities to read words. In terms of word features, words that were more frequently occurring were read better than less-frequent words (e.g., *the* vs. *enough*). In addition, the regularity of the words also influenced readers. Words that could be decoded using very common rules were easier to read (e.g., *cat* vs. *key*). Even with irregular words, students must use decoding skills and spelling knowledge along with vocabulary knowledge. It also confirms that word frequency and regularity are the two most influential impactors of irregular-word reading.

Teach Less-Regular Words with a Solid Grounding in Letter Sounds Along with Mispronunciation Correction (SfV)

In a synthesis, researchers reported the findings of eleven studies that directly compared different ways to teach students to read irregular words (Colenbrander et al. 2020). They identified three different approaches to irregular-word instruction: (a) sight-word instruction (e.g., look at it/visually memorize it with phonics); (b) mispronunciation correction (e.g., "Is that a word you know?"); and (c) morphology (e.g., look for meaningful word parts). In this review, sight-word instruction usually included some type of letter-sound analysis—hearing the word, seeing it, spelling it, visualizing it, and using pictures and/or mnemonics (Colenbrander et al. 2020).

Research on mispronunciation correction suggested that it was effective, but only in conjunction with letter-sound instruction. Because mispronunciation correction was always combined with letter-sound instruction, it was not possible to understand its singular impact. The data suggested advantages for having students test out different pronunciations when reading irregular words but noted that more research needed to be done. In terms of using morphology to support decoding irregular words, such as *two*, the data was inconsistent.

The authors end the article with the following statement: "In general, therefore, while there is not one clear answer to the question of how irregular words should be taught, we suggest that the best approach is to start with a solid grounding in grapheme-phoneme correspondence knowledge and introduce children to a small subset of high-frequency irregular words that they are unlikely to be able to decode accurately" (Colenbrander et al. 2020, 103).

All Words Eventually Become Sight Words Through Orthographic Mapping

An important research synthesis by prolific word recognition researcher Linnea Ehri describes the research studies that support the theory of sight-word recognition (Ehri 2005). A sight word is one that the reader accesses from memory automatically. Sight recognition is the most efficient way to read a word, and developing a large reservoir of words known by sight characterizes skilled readers. The studies overwhelmingly show that the process of learning sight words requires making connections between the letters and sounds and connecting the spellings to the pronunciations. This process is called *orthographic mapping* and applies even to irregular words.

Many of the studies reviewed by Ehri provide experimental support for the four phases of sight-word learning, phases that reflect increasing use of alphabetic information. These are (1) pre-alphabetic; (2) partial alphabetic; (3) full alphabetic; and (4) consolidated alphabetic. Each stage is differentiated by increasing application of alphabetic information to word reading. At the pre-alphabetic stage, a young reader might remember the visual shape of a word, its length, or even double letters, but not the connection to the sounds. As readers learn the letter sounds, they enter the partial alphabetic stage and can use beginning and ending letter sounds to recognize words. At the full alphabetic phase, readers can fully blend words because they know vowel sounds, and in the consolidated alphabetic phrase, readers know how to group letter sequences into patterns, syllables, or morphemes (e.g., –*ing*, *bas-ket*, *t-ea-m*).

Words that are decoded become orthographically mapped in the brain. That is, the word is remembered based on the letter-sound code and it becomes automatic. Regardless of whether the letter-sound correspondences are regular, less regular, or irregular, the same processes are used: connection between the letters and the sounds that the letters represent. For example, an irregular word such as *fuschia* would be mapped in this way: f /f/ + u /yoo/ + sch /sh/ + ia /ə/.

So What? Actions for the Classroom

Resist Drilling High-Frequency Words for Visual Memorization

The research evidence very clearly points to the fact that words that are learned and retained are orthographically mapped. Although it is possible to visually memorize a small set of words, that strategy will eventually wear out. If you remember the word *look* because it has two *o*'s, then you will think that words such as *book, took, hook, shook,* and many others are also *look*. Readers must know how the letters map to the sounds in words, even in less-regular words. We find teachers can get excited and deceived as children learn twenty or even thirty words visually, thinking that the strategy is working. Then, as the memory burden becomes too high and children can't retain the words, teachers become puzzled and frustrated.

This also means that unless children are being taught and know their letter sounds (not letter names), there is no reason to send home lists of high-frequency words. Lists of preschool sight words are usually not appropriate because most preschoolers do not know the majority of the letter sounds. The same might be said of lists going home for multilingual learners at the very early stages of acquiring English.

Teach High-Frequency Words Alongside Phonics Instruction

High-frequency word instruction should not take place in a vacuum but should be part of a comprehensive reading program that includes phonics instruction. This means that as students are learning high-frequency words, they are also learning letter-sound patterns in a systematic phonics program. Both phonics and high-frequency word learning are happening at the same time and are connected. This means that when you come to a new word, especially one for which students have learned patterns, you don't say, "Oh, this is a weird word. The letter sounds don't work, just memorize it." (See below for what to do in that situation.)

When a High-Frequency Word Has a Phoneme-Grapheme Pattern That Students Don't Know, Lightly Teach the Orthographic Mapping

In early reading instruction, teachers will often be in situations where students need to learn a high-frequency word before they have learned its patterns. For example, *her* is a very common word, but the r-controlled vowel pattern is not typically taught until much later in a phonics scope and sequence. So, what is a teacher to do? We suggest lightly mapping the orthography of the word. Show the children the match between the phonemes in the word and the letters, but realize that you are not teaching for mastery because *–er* will be taught in a more focused way later.

Where Possible, Group High-Frequency Words by Phoneme-Grapheme Patterns

Most word lists are organized by frequency—how often the word occurs. What this often means is that words with different patterns are grouped together, and this can be frustrating. For example, figure 8.1 below shows the high-frequency words listed in frequency order. Notice the pre-primer-level words, the first words taught, include *the*, *to*, *and*, *you*, and *said*. These words have complex and less-regular patterns. This order of words almost encourages visual memorization because there are no letter-sound consistencies among the words. Instead, the list of high frequency words in figure 8.2 (found at the Reading Rockets website) is grouped by spelling pattern.

When Students Mispronounce a Word, Ask, "Is That a Word You Know?"

The research on mispronunciation correction suggests that if a student mispronounces a word, it is a good idea to ask, "Is that a word you know?" Research tells us that cross-checking the pronunciation against a set of words helps students (Kearns et al. 2016). The procedure asks students to integrate decoding with the words they know. When their decoded words do not match words they know, then they can make adjustments.

Some high-frequency words have less-regular patterns, but due to their very common use in English, students will likely have these words in their spoken vocabularies. For example, a student might read *was* with an unvoiced /s/ sound (rhyming with *class*). Asking, "Is that a word you know?" is likely to bring up the correct pronunciation.

Figure 8.1 Dolch Words Grouped by Frequency, by Grade

Pre-primer	Primer	First	Second	Third
the	he	of	would	if
to	was	his	very	long
and	that	had	your	about
a	she	him	its	got
I	on	her	around	six
you	they	some	don't	never
it	but	as	right	seven
in	at	than	green	eight
said	with	could	their	today
for	all	when	call	myself
up	there	were	sleep	much
look	out	them	five	keep
is	be	ask	wash	try
go	have	an	or	start
we	am	over	before	ten
little	do	just	been	bring
down	did	from	off	drink
can	what	any	cold	only
see	so	how	tell	better

Figure 8.2 High Frequency Words Grouped by Spelling Pattern (Partial List)

VC (sorted by vowel spelling)	CVC (sorted by vowel spelling)	Digraphs (sorted by digraph)	Blends (sorted by ending blends, then beginning blends)	Words Ending in NG and NK (sorted by ending letters)
at (21)	had (20) hot (203)	that (14)	and (3)	sing (213)
am (37)	can (42) but (19)	with (23)	just (78)	bring (155)
an (72)	ran (111) run (163)	then (38)	must (149)	long (167)
it (8)	him (22) cut (188)	them (52)	fast (182)	thank (216)
in (10)	did (45) get (51)	this (55)	best (210)	think (110)
if (65)	will (59) yes (60)	much (142)	went (62)	drink (159)
on (17)	big (61) red (80)	pick (185)	ask (70)	
off (132)	six (120) well (109)	wish (217)	its (75)	
up (24)	sit (191) let (112)	when (44)	jump (98)	
us (169)	not (49) tell (141)	which (192)	help (113)	
	got (93) ten (153)		stop (131)	
			black (151)	

Source: Linda Farrell, Michael Hunter, and Tina Osenga, "A New Model for Teaching High Frequency Words." Reading Rockets. readingrockets.org/topics/phonics-and-decoding/articles/.

Practice High-Frequency Words in Phrases and Sentences as well as in Isolation

Many high-frequency words are what we might call function words (e.g., prepositions such as *to, for*; articles such as *a, an, the*; and auxiliary verbs such as *do, am, will*). In other words, they don't have an easily described meaning, outside of their use in sentences. A word like *cat* can be described and defined, but that's not so for a word like *to*. Often, the easiest way to help a student to understand these words is by using a phrase: "*to*, like *to the store*." It is always a good idea to practice reading words in multiple contexts so that students will generalize across situations. This is particularly the case with high-frequency words, because they are most meaningful within sentences and phrases. Understanding the meaning of a word contributes to decoding it.

How should I teach high-frequency sight words?

DO	DON'T
• Teach alongside phonics. • Orthographically map the word even if the pattern has yet to be taught. • Ask the student: "Is that a word you know?" • Organize by pattern.	• Teach without phonics. • Encourage visual memorization. • Tell students: "It doesn't make sense." • Call high-frequency words "sight words."

Other Useful Resources

Dolch, E. W. 1936. "A Basic Sight Vocabulary." *The Elementary School Journal* 36 (6): 456–460.

Fry, E. 1980. "The New Instant Word List." *The Reading Teacher* 34 (3): 284–289.

Kearns, D. M., H. J. Rogers, T. Koriakin, and R. Al Ghanem. 2016. "Semantic and Phonological Ability to Adjust Recoding: A Unique Correlate of Word Reading Skill?" *Scientific Studies of Reading* 20 (6): 455–470.

Question 9

Is invented spelling supported by research? Is it damaging to children's later reading and writing?

Discussion from the Classroom

Tina, a kindergarten teacher in a charter school in an urban center, uses journal writing in her kindergarten classroom. But recently, after attending several workshops focusing on the Science of Reading, she began to have questions about the invented spelling that children produced as they wrote and illustrated simple sentences.

"Travon was writing about Christmas and spelled it like this: *ksmss*. I thought that was pretty good. He represented several of the consonant sounds, even though he used *k* for the /k/ sound, not *ch*. But then I got to thinking, am I encouraging low standards? Is he going to think that this is the way you write *Christmas*? Should I have gone in and showed him how to spell it correctly and asked him to copy it over?"

Many teachers have questions like this and want to know more about what the research really says about invented spelling. They are worried that they will be called out for not correcting misspellings or worse, that they could be damaging their students.

Background and Assumptions

Invented spelling: This is spelling students use when they have incomplete knowledge of the phoneme-grapheme patterns in English (typically in grades preK–1). Invented spellings are not random (e.g., *asdfsafdxc*) but reflect the alphabetic principle with logical substitutions, such as in these examples:

→ missing vowels in unaccented parts of multisyllabic words (e.g., *Christmas = ksmss*)

→ missing consonants in blends (e.g., *trap = tap*)

- substitutions based on letter names (e.g., *why* = *Y*)
- substitutions based on similar place and manner of sound's articulation (e.g., *field* = *vid*)
- single letters to spell words based on phonemic insights (e.g., *dog* = *D*).

Temporary, accountable, phonetic, phonological, or **logical spelling:** Some educators use other terms for invented spelling. *Phonetic* and *phonological spelling* reflects that children are spelling words as they sound (Ehri and Wilce 1987). The term *temporary* implies that the attempt is not to be accepted later as the student develops (Kemeny 2023). *Logical* spelling points to the thoughtful application of known phoneme-grapheme correspondences. *Accountable* spelling suggests that students should be accountable for their spelling attempts and that the teacher should ask them to make corrections for patterns that they have been taught.

Research Studies That Inform the Question

Møller, H. L., J. O. Mortensen, and C. Elbro. 2022. "Effects of Integrated Spelling in Phonics Instruction for At-Risk Children in Kindergarten." *Reading & Writing Quarterly* 38 (1): 67–82.

Ouellette, G., and M. Sénéchal. 2008. "Pathways to Literacy: A Study of Invented Spelling and Its Role in Learning to Read." *Child Development* 79 (4): 899–913.

Ouellette, G., M. Sénéchal, and A. Haley. 2013. "Guiding Children's Invented Spellings: A Gateway into Literacy Learning." *The Journal of Experimental Education* 81 (2): 261–279.

Sénéchal, M., G. Ouellette, and H. N. L. Nguyen. 2023. "Invented Spelling: An Integrative Review of Descriptive, Correlational, and Causal Evidence." In *Handbook on the Science of Early Literacy*, edited by S. Q. Cabell, S. B. Neuman, and N. P. Terry, 95–106. New York: Guilford.

Research Findings

Invented Spelling Occurs in Research-Based Developmental Stages

Although in this Science of Reading era we encounter many who believe that invented spelling is a whole-language free-for-all that should be avoided, as it turns out, invented spelling is supported by the research, but not exactly in the way that most teachers think about it. In the recently released *Handbook of the Science of Early Literacy*, there is a meta-analysis on invented spelling (Sénéchal, Ouellette, Nguyen 2023). The chapter titled "Invented Spelling: An Integrative Review of Descriptive, Correlational, and Causal

Evidence" reviews the research on invented spelling in three areas: (a) descriptions of developmental stages; (b) predictions of later spelling, reading, and decoding based on invented spelling (meta-analysis); and (c) experimental or training studies that used invented spelling to improve outcomes (meta-analysis). Most studies were conducted in kindergarten.

Imagine a kindergartner is asked to spell the word *strike*. The research review described the developmental progression in invented spelling:

a. first sound—*s*
b. first + last sound—*sc* or *sk*
c. first + last + vowel—*sik* or *suc*
d. first + last + vowel + consonant blend—*stik* or *sric* or *strik*
e. first + last + vowel + blend + vowel marker—*stike* or *stryk*

Developmental research shows that students may use graphemes that are inaccurate but that do represent the target sound (e.g., *k/c*) and that vowel sounds may be present but not accurate (e.g., *i/u*).

Invented Spelling Interventions Mediate Accurate Spelling, Letter Learning, Phonemic Awareness, and Word Reading

In the previously mentioned meta-analysis, findings showed that when instruction used invented spelling to inform feedback, there was an impact on accurate spelling (.48 effect size) and word reading (.43 effect size) (Sénéchal, Ouellette, and Nguyen 2023).

In an experiment conducted in Denmark, researchers randomly assigned sixty-five kindergarten children to one of four conditions: (1) No treatment (control); (2) Integrated Spelling (Invented Spelling); (3) Letter-Sound Production; and (4) Letter-Sound Recognition.

Children learned nine letter sounds over four sessions of twenty minutes each and practiced reading words at the end of the lessons (Møller, Mortensen, and Elbro 2022). For the Integrated Spelling condition, words with the taught letter sounds were dictated, and participants used letter cards to spell the words. The words all had two to three letters and were regular words. The instructor orally pronounced each word one time. Children segmented the word orally and then chose letter tiles to spell the word. In the Letter-Sound Production condition, participants practiced producing the sounds represented by letters in games. In the Letter-Sound Recognition condition, the participants practiced pointing to the correct letters for sounds after the instructor said each sound.

For an intervention that was only four days and eighty minutes long, results were impressive! Not only did the Integrated Spelling group learn the letters, but they also outperformed all of the groups in phoneme analysis, spelling the words, and reading new words that they had not been taught.

In another series of studies, researchers tested the causal role between using invented spelling and feedback and later reading (Ouellette and Sénéchal 2008; Ouellette, Sénéchal, and Haley 2013). In the first study, kindergartners were randomly assigned to either an invented-spelling group or a phonological-awareness group (Ouellette and Sénéchal 2008). This four-week intervention helped students' phonological awareness and their abilities to read words in the training. But most interestingly, students in the invented-spelling group were better able to learn to decode new words that they had never seen before. The challenge of attempting to spell words seemingly advanced their abilities to decode.

The second study was very similar, with forty kindergartners randomly assigned to the same two treatments but for a longer period. As in the first study, students in the invented-spelling group were also better able to learn to read new words (Ouellette, Sénéchal, and Haley 2013).

Why do the effects of invented spelling interventions impact other behaviors? It seems that this statement sums it up: "Students see spellings as maps of phonemic content rather than an arbitrary sequence of letters. Practice in using the alphabetic strategy to spell words seems to transfer to reading words" (Gersten et al. 2008, 29).

So What? Actions for the Classroom

Use Invented Spelling, Especially in Kindergarten and Early First Grade

If there is anything to take away from the invented spelling research, it is this: Simply asking students to do invented spelling is not enough. We like to say, "Students *do it*. Teachers *use it*."

After reading this research, we both came away with the understanding that for some time, we had a fundamental misinterpretation. We thought that children using invented spelling was enough. We thought that transcribing speech into print formed the sum of what made invented spelling impactful. In fact, the research tells us that invented spelling caused changes in spelling and word reading *only when teachers provided feedback.*

Make Invented Spelling Part of Your Daily Letter and Decoding Instruction

We are learning so much about letter instruction in kindergarten, and the work on invented spelling shows that teachers should consider including invented spelling as they are teaching letters. In these studies, kindergartners learning their first letters dove right into spelling. Importantly, they began to just write words with two sounds and then words with three sounds (Møller, Mortensen, and Elbro 2022). When you are teaching letters, sweep away the visual prompts, stretch out short words, and ask children to spell.

Just do it! Do it every day as you are teaching letters and decoding. Analyzing a word and decoding is only part of the equation. Use the additional directions below.

Model How to Spell a Word, Then Let Students Try It

Most kindergarten teachers understand that simply asking students to spell words is not enough. Students will need a process to use, something to turn to as they try. Here are some steps that reflect the research:

1.	Say the word and then stretch the phonemes in the word.	"bag" "baaaaaagg"
2.	Ask the students to say the word and stretch it. Some teachers will also count the sounds after stretching them. This is especially useful with three- and four-phoneme words.	"bag" "baaaaaagg"
3.	Model transcribing the sounds using an alphabet chart for support.	"/b/. How do we spell /b/? Let me look on my alphabet chart. Oh! *b*! I will write it."
4.	Model checking. Stretch the word, matching the sounds to the letters written.	"/b/ /a/ ___(child left out *g*). Oh, I have two sounds but I forgot one."

Without this process that illustrates the phonemic nature of sound-spelling correspondences, students will think that spelling is copying or will badger everyone around them with "How do you spell _____?" When you empower students with a strategy and you ask them to spell sounds for which they have been taught the letters, they can do it.

Assess Invented Spellings

Students will move beyond learning letters and into decoding and spelling the many vowel patterns that they see in words. At this time, daily spelling is a good way to see what is sticking with your students. Let's say it's March and you have a group of kindergartners who have been learning the closed-syllable pattern with short *a*. You ask them to spell *nap* and notice that Hunter writes *nep* and Taylor writes *np*. The developmental literature would tell you that Taylor is not really noticing the middle sound, even if you are teaching it. So, some reteaching and phonemic awareness on middle sounds is needed. Hunter, however, has a vowel, but just needs to get it right. So, isolating the middle sound and then sending him to an alphabet chart would work: "Hmmm, let's do our roller coaster: *naaaap*. Hold it in the middle: *naaaa*. What do you hear? Look at your alphabet chart. Is that the letter e or a?"

Ask for More: Provide Feedback Based on Spelling and the Developmental Literature

Because of our own misperceptions, we often focused on first attempts at invented spelling as the end game. But really, that's not what the research says. Once students get something down, the teacher should quickly analyze the attempt, then offer feedback based on the developmental literature. The idea is that invented spelling provides a tool that the teacher can use to gently advance a child's knowledge. So, if a child spells the first sound in a word accurately, the teacher would press for a final sound, perhaps stretching the word, emphasizing the last sound, and then asking the child to attempt that last sound. If the invented spelling has the first and last sounds but not a vowel, a teacher might press to listen for the middle sound and get that in the word.

Cautions and Caveats

- Most invented spelling research has been conducted with kindergartners.
- A few of the studies on invented spelling were conducted in alphabetic languages other than English (e.g., Danish, Hebrew), but invented spelling research applies to any alphabetic spelling.
- Expressive writing, or children creating their own messages, should also be a regular part of instruction. During these times, children will attempt to spell words phonetically for which they do not know all the patterns (e.g., *strolbares* = *strawberries*). It is amazing what children will work for when the message is theirs!
- Invented spelling is not random spelling. Invented spelling is an application of the alphabetic principle–based knowledge that students are gaining.

Is invented spelling supported by research?

Invented spelling interventions in kindergarten ARE research supported.
(also called *phonetic, phonological,* or *temporary spelling*)

It's not enough for kids to just "do" invented spelling. It's a starting place.

Give feedback on the process:

- How to spell a word: *Let's stretch it. How many sounds? How do I spell that sound?*

Give tailored feedback, based on sounds represented:

- Is the first sound present? Push for the final sound. *Listen for the last sound: cttttt. You say it. What sound is at the end? How do you spell that?*
- Are first and final sounds present? Push for a vowel. *Let's stretch it and hold in the middle: caaaat. You say it. Hold it in the middle. What sound is that? How do you spell that?*
- Are all sounds present? Push for conventional spelling: *kat* to *cat.*

Children do it. Teachers use it.

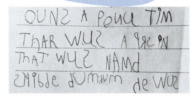

Effect Sizes

.43 on word reading

.48 on later correct spelling

(Sénéchal, Ouellette, and Nguyen 2023)

Other Useful Resources

Gersten, R., D. Compton, C. M. Connor, J. Dimino, L. Santoro, S. Linan-Thompson, and W. D. Till. 2008. *Assisting Students Struggling with Reading: Response to Intervention and Multi-Tier Intervention for Reading in the Primary Grades. A Practice Guide.* (NCEE 2009-4045). National Center for Education Evaluation and Regional Assistance, Institute of Education Sciences, U.S. Department of Education. ies.ed.gov/ncee/wwc/Docs/PracticeGuide/rti_reading_pg_021809.pdf.

Question 10

Kids spend so much time on phones and computers, do they really need to be taught handwriting?

Discussion from the Classroom

Handwriting is not in vogue in many schools. Because it is viewed as a kind of mechanistic, low-level skill, often schools are not giving enough attention to it. This might be a reaction to previous eras when handwriting took large amounts of instruction time and young children too often were frustrated by tediously perfecting letters. It also might be a reflection of the fact that keyboards dominate our world. Why learn how to handwrite if you are going to be typing or texting for most of your life?

Recently, when Heidi Anne was in a school, she experienced a situation that illustrated what research is increasingly showing—that handwriting instruction is essential. She watched a young kindergartner become frustrated, and eventually give up, as he tried to write in his journal. Full of great ideas and the letter-sound knowledge to help him spell the words, he was slowed down by poor pencil grip and an idiosyncratic approach to forming letters. When he made a lowercase *b*, for instance, he formed it differently each time, with no consistency. He might start at the bottom and move up one time and then another time start with the circle. In addition, his letters were not very legible. His *q* looked like an *a*. This child needed some handwriting instruction, not only for fluency and legibility but also to integrate his letter-sound knowledge with the physical actions required to form letters.

Background and Assumptions

The Simple View of Writing identifies four elements of creating a written message: text generation, transcription, working memory, and executive function (Berninger and Amtmann 2003). Handwriting falls under transcription. Specifically, handwriting is defined as "a complex task requiring the coordination of several cognitive, motoric, and neuromotor processes" (Dinehart 2015, 99). Handwriting requires fine-motor skills, hand-eye coordination, and muscle memory.

Handwriting includes two equally important parts: legibility and fluency. Legible handwriting is writing in which the letters are clear and accurate and the message easily read. Fluency refers to handwriting that is produced at a sufficient rate of speed with sufficient motor control and coordination of fine-motor skills so as to be smooth and automatically rendered.

Research Studies That Inform the Question

Engel, C., K. Lillie, S. Zurawski, and B. G. Travers. 2018. "Curriculum-Based Handwriting Programs: A Systematic Review with Effect Sizes." *The American Journal of Occupational Therapy* 72 (3): 7203205010p1–7203205010p8. doi.org/10.5014/ajot.2018.027110.

Feng, L., A. Lindner, X. R. Ji, and R. Malatesha Joshi. 2019. "The Roles of Handwriting and Keyboarding in Writing: A Meta-Analytic Review." *Reading and Writing* 32 (1): 33–63.

Pritchard, V. E., S. A. Malone, and C. Hulme. 2021. "Early Handwriting Ability Predicts the Growth of Children's Spelling, but Not Reading, Skills." *Scientific Studies of Reading* 25 (4): 304–331.

Ray, K., K. Dally, K. Colyvas, and A. E. Lane. 2021. "The Effects of a Whole-Class Kindergarten Handwriting Intervention on Early Reading Skills." *Reading Research Quarterly* 56 (S1): S193–S207.

Santangelo, T., and S. Graham. 2016. "A Comprehensive Meta-Analysis of Handwriting Instruction." *Educational Psychology Review* 28 (2): 225–265.

Research Findings ←←←←

Handwriting Instruction Improves Legibility and Fluency of Writing and Quality of Written Expression

Across several meta-analyses and studies, researchers have found that handwriting instruction improves the legibility of handwriting, the speed of handwriting (e.g., number of letters written per minute), and the overall quality of written expression (Engel et al. 2018; Feng et al. 2019; Santangelo and Graham 2016). The quality of written expression is the "written substance of the paper including factors such as grammar, imagination, organization, and word choice" (Feng et al. 2019, 41). No relationship exists between complexity of writing (e.g., syntax, clause density) and handwriting fluency.

Essentially, research tell us that handwriting instruction has both direct effects on handwriting itself and generalizable effects on messaging. Students write more clearly so that others can understand their messages and more efficiently so that they are not slowed down by transcribing their thoughts. What's more, these improvements in speed and clarity impact the quality of their written expression. It's as if improving the mechanics of handwriting frees students to craft better messages. There may have been a trade-off between speed and legibility, because as legibility increased, speed decreased (Engel et al. 2018).

Handwriting Instruction Includes Specific Instructional Features

One of the biggest misconceptions about handwriting instruction is that it consists of having children look at and copy letters, using their own approaches to form manuscript letters. Often developed by occupational therapists, high-quality handwriting instruction usually delineates consistent strokes in a particular order for efficient and fluid letter formation, minimizing the number of times a pencil must be lifted.

High-quality handwriting instruction models the way to hold a pencil, where to start letters in relation to lines on the paper, the strokes to take as the letter is made, and the order in which those strokes are made (Ray et al. 2021). Instruction can be delivered to the whole group and includes formation lessons that contain mnemonics to remember how to form each letter (e.g., strokes for lowercase a = around, up, and down). Importantly, good instruction also involves repeated practice writing the letters. In some studies, generic fine-motor instruction and/or skills were coupled with handwriting instruction (e.g., making lines and circles), but these generic fine-motor skills were not found to have an impact (Pritchard, Malone, and Hulme 2021; Santangelo and Graham 2016). Lastly, individualized handwriting instruction positively impacted legibility and may be needed for some students (Santangelo and Graham 2016).

Instructional elements that did not impact handwriting instruction included: (a) motion models; (b) motor instruction (e.g., teaching how to make lines and circles); (c) self-evaluation; (d) multisensory features; and (e) copying letters (Santangelo and Graham 2016).

Handwriting Contributes to Letter Learning, Acquisition of the Alphabetic Principle, and Word Reading

Many people think of handwriting as a lower-order mechanical skill that reflects rather than contributes to early literacy skills such as letter naming, letter-sound recognition, or word reading. In other words, handwriting is not thought of as influencing or improving early literacy skills. However, the research tells us that learning to write letters actually mediates, or supports, letter learning, spelling, and word reading in the future (Pritchard, Malone, and Hulme 2021; Ray et al. 2021). In an experiment with kindergartners, an interdisciplinary team of reading researchers and occupational therapists tested the impact of a four-part instructional model addressing the following factors: (a) recall, or remembering the letter from memory; (b) retrieval, or doing the system of motor movements; (c) reproduction, or factors enhancing handwriting—fine motor, visual motor, visuoperceptual; and (d) repetition, or practice. The program caused better letter-naming (but not letter-sound) knowledge and word reading. A longitudinal study found that variations in handwriting skills influenced growth in spelling but not word reading (Pritchard, Malone, and Hulme 2021). Why does handwriting aid coding skills? Researchers hypothesize that motor-perceptual links that are required for handwriting "seal" all facets of letter information in memory, adding a kinesthetic path.

Handwriting Curricula Enhance Legibility and Speed

Several studies analyzed the effects of handwriting curricula on legibility, writing fluency, and writing quality (Engel et al. 2018; Santangelo and Graham 2016). A meta-analysis published in *The American Journal of Occupational Therapy* (Engel et al. 2018) identified thirteen studies examining the effects of nine different handwriting programs. Eight of the thirteen improved handwriting legibility in preschool–early elementary students, and five of the thirteen improved handwriting speed. Most programs improved legibility in about six weeks, but students with higher needs may need more time. Importantly, these programs were all evaluated by occupational therapists, who are essential partners in handwriting improvement.

So What? Actions for the Classroom

Systematically Teach Handwriting, Applying Research-Based Elements

Just like any other part of the literacy curriculum, handwriting instruction must be conducted in a systematic and purposeful way. This starts with a planned scope and sequence of the letters to be taught and the steps to teaching them. Teachers can organize their own plan or use research-based curricula. Giving students paper and pencil and asking them to copy letters is not handwriting instruction any more than giving a child a book is reading instruction. Handwriting instruction starts with showing students how to hold the pencil between the thumb and forefingers. Instruction for writing a given letter begins with a visual diagram of the letter strokes, modeling the strokes of the letter in relationship to the lines on the paper, and guiding practice of the letter at least five to eight times. Follow-up instruction should include a gradual release of responsibility in which students write letters from memory without diagrams and apply letter writing in words, sentences, and stories. Handwriting is amenable to whole-group instruction several times a week, with individualized follow-up for students who need it. Because it is a motor skill, multiple short sessions across a week are best. At least six weeks of instruction are needed for the effects of handwriting instruction to be seen. When first learning, students will need extra time because there is a trade-off between legible, accurate letters and speed. Accuracy in any skill precedes fluency or speed. Fortunately, well-designed writing strokes will optimize efficiency so that students eventually automatize handwriting with little thought to mechanics.

Integrate Handwriting with Alphabet and Other Code Instruction

Although the Science of Reading and the Science of Writing are often not well integrated, recent research has demonstrated that handwriting instruction mediates or enhances code skills. So, it should be a regular part of alphabet instruction and spelling. Although focused handwriting instruction will have its own time in the day, when reviewing letters or teaching new ones, the handwriting strokes for a letter can be included. Children can air-write or quickly practice writing a letter as they are reviewing its sound. During activities and games that involve spelling, a quick review of the proper way to make a letter should take place. Bring the handwriting piece into code instruction for extra review and practice that reinforces making letters properly.

Work with an Occupational Therapist

Classroom teachers are used to being lone rangers, but when it comes to handwriting, they should enlist the assistance of an occupational therapist (OT). Occupational therapists have specific expertise in understanding and supporting the development of the specific fine-motor skills that undergird handwriting. In other words, they know what to expect from a five-year-old, and they have tips and tricks to help with pencil grip and memory for handwriting strokes. Further, they will also know how to make it fun! In addition, OTs will know how to help with common problems that may come up, such as left-handed students, students struggling with fine-motor skills, and ways to alleviate fatigue. If it is not possible to have an OT co-teach at least once a week, then sit down with this expert before teaching, and consult them throughout your handwriting unit.

Do kids really need to be taught handwriting?

Handwriting ≠ copying letters

- Handwriting *mediates* letter learning, spelling, and word reading.
- Short sessions prevent fatigue.
- Efficient, consistent strokes save time and energy.
- Partner with an occupational therapist.

Initial Instruction

1. Have a plan, use a curriculum.
2. Dedicate time.
3. Teach pencil grip.
4. Use diagrams.
5. Model strokes.
6. Offer guided practice five to eight times.

Follow-up

- Write letters from memory.
- At least six weeks of instruction.
- Individualize for some students.

(Engel et al. 2018; Pritchard et al. 2021; Ray et al. 2021; Santagelo and Graham 2016)

Cautions and Caveats

→ There are very few, if any, randomized controlled trials of existing handwriting curriculum or studies that randomly assigned students to different handwriting programs and tested the effects (Engel et al. 2018).

Other Useful Resources

Berninger, V. W., and D. Amtmann. 2003. "Preventing Written Expression Disabilities Through Early and Continuing Assessment and Intervention for Handwriting and/or Spelling Problems: Research into Practice." In *Handbook of Learning Disabilities* (1st ed.), edited by H. L. Swanson, K. R. Harris, and S. Graham, 345–363. New York: Guilford.

Dinehart, L. H. 2015. "Handwriting in Early Childhood Education: Current Research and Future Implications." *Journal of Early Childhood Literacy* 15 (1): 97–118.

PART 2

Language and Other Skills Supporting COMPREHENSION

Question 11

For oral reading practice, should students read the same text repeatedly or read different texts?

Discussion from the Classroom

Recently, in one of our graduate-level reading classes, an interesting discussion about the benefits of repeated reading took place among elementary teachers. The discussion began with a lively debate about repeated oral reading:

> "The research clearly supports repeated reading as the go-to for improving fluency. There are all these articles that tell you to have students reread the same passage and time it and even computer programs that help you set that up," explained Marcia, a second grade teacher.

> "Yeah, but it gets so boring," replied Dale, "and then they pick up on the timing and just start speed reading, which kind of defeats the point. I know repeated oral reading is research-based, but I wonder about what it is really accomplishing."

> "We've also read about the benefits of wide reading on vocabulary. Does it matter if students are rereading the same text, or is it better to have students read multiple texts? Our goal is ultimately to improve reading comprehension. Time is limited in the classroom," added Ashley, a fourth grade teacher.

Background and Assumptions

Repeated oral reading, where students reread the same passage multiple times, can be really useful, especially when students are reading texts with unfamiliar, complex vocabulary. Repeated oral reading can also build the confidence of striving readers because they can track their improvement as a result of reading more challenging passages. Another way to build fluency is to have students do the same amount of reading, but with a variety of passages, which is known as *continuous reading* (O'Connor, White, and Swanson 2007). Continuous reading, also known as wide reading, may be more interesting for students, and it still gives them a great deal of practice. Continuous reading also more closely mirrors the type of reading that people do outside of school. However, the passages in continuous reading have a larger range of words. In the discussion above, the teachers questioned whether it is better to have students reread the same text repeatedly or to have them practice by reading widely from a number of texts. Below, we summarize research comparing two instructional approaches to repeated reading and corroborate the research findings with a third study that focused on struggling readers in second and fourth grades. (Struggling readers were defined as having a low reading rate on grade-level pages and a score greater than 69 on the Peabody Picture Vocabulary Test–Third Edition (PPVT-III).)

Research Studies That Inform the Question

Kuhn, M. R., P. J. Schwanenflugel, R. D. Morris, L. M. Morrow, D. G. Woo, E. B. Meisinger, R. A. Sevcik, B. A. Bradley, and S. A. Stahl. 2006. "Teaching Children to Become Fluent and Automatic Readers." *Journal of Literacy Research* 38 (4): 357–387.

O'Connor, R. E., A. White, and H. L. Swanson. 2007. "Repeated Reading versus Continuous Reading: Influences on Reading Fluency and Comprehension." *Exceptional Children* 74 (1): 31–46.

Stahl, S. A., and K. Heubach. 2005. "Fluency-Oriented Reading Instruction." *Journal of Literacy Research* 37 (1): 25–60.

Research Findings

Fluency-Oriented Reading Instruction (FORI) and Wide-Reading Instruction

Fluency-Oriented Reading Instruction (FORI) (Stahl and Heubach 2005) involves whole-class instruction with teacher modeling and students rereading the same grade-level text across the week. (See Figure 11.1 for a suggested weekly schedule.) Typically, students read a text between four and seven times over the course of a week. Kuhn and colleagues contrasted FORI with a wide-reading approach, which incorporates many of the same principles as FORI, such as modeling and rereading. However, in the wide-reading approach, students read three grade-level texts across the week instead of a single text repeatedly (Kuhn et al. 2006). (See Figure 11.1 for a comparison of the two approaches.)

The first two days of instruction are similar in both FORI and the wide-reading approach. The teacher introduces the first text and models reading as students follow along. On Day 2, students echo-read the text practiced on the first day. In the wide-reading approach, students participate in extension activities on Day 3. Then, instead of rereading the same text on Days 4 and 5 as in FORI, students echo-read and discuss two new texts. In this wide-rereading approach, students typically reread the first text between two and four times and then read the secondary texts only once or twice.

Regular Practice Reading Text Aloud Matters

Unsurprisingly, in a yearlong study in second grade classrooms, FORI (repeated reading) and the wide-reading approach (combination of rereading and continuous reading) significantly increased the amount of time each week that students spent reading orally through choral-, echo-, and partner-reading. This oral reading was associated with significant positive growth in measures of word recognition, fluency, and comprehension (Kuhn et al. 2006). A second study of second and fourth grade struggling readers similarly found that reading aloud for fifteen minutes three times a week for fourteen weeks led to improved word recognition, reading rate, and comprehension (O'Connor, White, and Swanson 2007).

Wide and Repeated Reading Both Positively Impact Word Recognition and Comprehension

Surprisingly, when measuring automatic word recognition, it did not matter whether students read one text repeatedly (FORI) or three texts across the week (wide reading). Students participating in wide-reading classrooms experienced gains in automatic word reading earlier when compared to the FORI group. Wide reading also promoted text fluency over the FORI condition (Kuhn et al. 2006). (Passage-reading accuracy and speed and text fluency were measured using the Gray Oral Reading Test, 4th edition, and automatic word recognition was measured using the TOWRE assessment.) Students in the rereading and continuous reading conditions did equally well on fluency and comprehension measures in O'Connor, White, and Swanson's study (2007). Both oral reading practice conditions resulted in positive growth, and one condition was not more effective than the other. The authors concluded, "Given the current evidence, practice reading aloud with corrective feedback appears to be more important than the specific model of practice" (44).

So What? Actions for the Classroom

Incorporate Both Wide Reading and Repeated Reading (But Wide Reading May Offer Several Advantages)

The authors of the *IES Practice Guide for Foundational Skills* recommend both repeated reading and wide reading, stating advantages of both: "In repeated reading, students are less likely to practice incorrect word reading or to guess unknown words. They are repeatedly exposed to the same words, which should help students recognize them more efficiently. Wide reading, on the other hand, exposes students to more diverse vocabulary and word knowledge" (Foorman et al. 2016, 36).

Comparatively, both FORI and wide reading equally improve students' automatic word recognition and comprehension. While additional research is needed to replicate across grade levels and student factors, given the benefits associated with wide reading (such as vocabulary and comprehension), we generally agree with Kuhn, Rasinski, and Young (2013) who said they recommend the wide-reading approach when planning for whole-class fluency instruction, noting that it combines repeated reading and continuous reading. The wide-reading approach provides the best of both worlds. Instead of arguing about whether it is better to read for depth (repeated reading) or for breadth (continuous reading), we would shift perspectives and argue that reading for depth *and* for breadth are both important. This is what the wide-reading model provides. Students reread a focal text a few times before moving onto reading other related texts.

Use Research-Based Best Practices for Repeated Reading

→ We know that repeated reading works best when students receive corrective feedback when they read (O'Connor, White, and Swanson 2007).

→ Providing a model of fluent reading of the text in advance is also beneficial. Interestingly, this fluent model can come in many forms and does not require the teacher to do the modeling, rather a fluent reading by a peer, paraeducator, or even a recorded text can all provide effective models.

→ Allow opportunities for sustained, regular practice. Across the three studies, the oral reading practice lasted a minimum of fifteen minutes a day. "That means the texts need to be long enough for your students to read for an extended period of time (between 20 and 40 minutes per day) and that they are sufficiently challenging for your learners" (Kuhn, Rasinski, and Young 2013, 281).

Figure 11.1 Weekly Schedule Comparing the FORI and Wide-Reading Models of Oral Reading

WEEKLY MODEL OF FLUENCY-ORIENTED READING INSTRUCTION (Stahl and Heubach 2005; Kuhn et al. 2006)	WEEKLY MODEL OF WIDE-READING INSTRUCTION (Kuhn et al. 2006)
Day 1: • Teacher introduces and pre-teaches a new text. • Teacher reads the text aloud with students following along on their copies. • Teacher leads a brief, comprehension-focused discussion of the text.	**Day 1:** • Teacher introduces and pre-teaches a new text. • Teacher reads the text aloud with students following along on their copies. • Teacher leads a brief, comprehension-focused discussion of the text.
Day 2: • Teacher and students echo-read the text, two or three sentences at a time. • Students complete text-based activities. • Students practice reading the text at home.	**Day 2:** • Teacher and students echo-read the text, two or three sentences at a time. • Students practice reading the text at home.
Day 3: • The entire class chorally reads the text with the teacher.	**Day 3:** • Students complete text-based activities.
Day 4: • Students partner-read the text, taking turns. (Partners can be at the same skill level or a more skilled reader can be partnered with a less skilled peer.)	**Day 4:** • Students echo-read and discuss a second text.
Day 5: • Students complete additional activities related to the text.	**Day 5:** • Students echo-read and discuss a third text.

For oral reading practice, should students read the same text repeatedly or read different texts?

Fluency-Oriented Reading Instruction (FORI)

MONDAY	TUESDAY	WEDNESDAY	THURSDAY	FRIDAY

Wide-Reading Instruction (Wide-FORI)

MONDAY	TUESDAY	WEDNESDAY	THURSDAY	FRIDAY

Fluency instruction should include:
- Sustained, regular practice
- Corrective feedback
- Models of fluent reading
- Wide and repeated reading of texts

(Kuhn et. al 2006)

Other Useful Resources

Foorman, B., N. Beyler, K. Borradaile, M. Coyne, C. A. Denton, J. Dimino, J. Furgeson, L. Hayes, J. Henke, L. Justice, B. Keating, W. Lewis, S. Sattar, A. Streke, R. Wagner, and S. Wissel. 2016. *Foundational Skills to Support Reading for Understanding in Kindergarten Through 3rd Grade* (NCEE 2016-4008). National Center for Education Evaluation and Regional Assistance (NCEE), Institute of Education Sciences, U.S. Department of Education. ies.ed.gov/ncee/wwc/practiceguide/21.

Kuhn, M. R., T. Rasinski, and C. Young. 2013. "Best Practices in Fluency Instruction." In *Best Practices in Literacy Instruction* (6th ed.), edited by L. M. Morrow and L. B. Gambrell, 271–288. New York: Guilford.

Question 12

What types of texts should we use when working on reading with expression?

Discussion from the Classroom

Think about a recent conversation you've had. The message you were communicating was conveyed not only through the words you used but also how you used them. Consider the two-word phrase "That's interesting." Depending on the context and the speaker's tone, the sentence may convey fascination, curiosity, confusion, or even sarcasm. For instance, someone might say, "That's interesting" in a flat tone to convey sarcasm when a colleague drones on about their pet's finicky dietary needs. Contrast this to "That's interesting?" with a raised pitch at the end. This same phrase now sounds like a question. When reading orally, we must fluctuate different aspects of our voice in order to appropriately convey the author's message and tone. When we modulate our voice to maintain meaning, we are reading with appropriate expression, which is one of the main components of fluency identified by the National Reading Panel (NICHD 2000). *Prosody* refers to reading "with appropriate expression or intonation coupled with phrasing that allows for the maintenance of meaning" (Kuhn et al. 2010, 233).

According to the annual "What's Hot in Literacy" survey, fluency is not currently hot (Grote-Garcia and Ortlieb 2023). This is perhaps not surprising given the recent increased scrutiny and attention being paid to phonics and phonemic awareness. Given the popularity of the Simple View of Reading, elementary teachers may be wondering about the benefits of teaching reading with expression to their readers. Should we still dedicate classroom time to prosody? And if so, what types of texts should we use for prosody practice?

Background and Assumptions

Prosody consists of loudness, duration, pitch, and pausing (Benjamin and Schwanenflugel 2010).

- **Loudness:** When someone reads aloud, they add nuanced meaning when they loudly emphasize certain words or end in a hushed tone.

- **Duration:** Readers also emphasize or alter the meaning of words by stretching them out. (Have you ever heard a teenager stretch the word "mom" out to three syllables to indicate exasperation?) Duration also includes the rhythm of reading. A good limerick rests on the reader's ability to read with appropriate rhythm.

- **Pitch:** Readers indicate whether sentences are questions or statements by raising or lowering the pitch of their voice at the ends of sentences. *Intonation* is another term for pitch.

- **Pausing:** Finally, good readers tend to align their pausing with meaning phrases and syntax or grammar. They also pause to indicate a change in speakers when reading dialogue.

Prosody often gets overlooked by teachers because it has historically been difficult to assess. Traditional teacher fluency scales often combine multiple components of fluency, including accuracy and speed with expression, into a single measure. In such teacher ratings, it is often unclear whether low ratings are due to poor word recognition or low reading expression (Benjamin and Schwanenflugel 2010; Schwanenflugel et al. 2004). However, prosody serves as a bridge between word recognition and comprehension (Young, Paige, and Rasinski 2022; Duke and Cartwright 2021). When we read something with accuracy, appropriate speed and pausing, pitch, duration, and loudness, we are clearly comprehending what we read. And this comprehension is the very point of reading. Below, we explore the role of prosody and why it may contribute to comprehension independently of automatic word recognition.

Research Studies That Inform the Question

Benjamin, R. G., and P. J. Schwanenflugel. 2010. "Text Complexity and Oral Reading Prosody in Young Readers." *Reading Research Quarterly* **45 (4): 388–404.**

Research Findings

Benjamin and Schwanenflugel measured ninety second graders' prosody as they read easy (highly decodable) and difficult texts (readability of 3.79 grade level) to determine the effects of text complexity on prosody (2010). These prosody measures were then used as predictors of measures of speed and accuracy combined and comprehension. Instead of relying on teacher prosody ratings, the researchers used spectographic measurements to analyze students' reading prosody. (Spectograms are visual displays of speech that researchers can analyze to study various components of prosody.) They measured pitch, intonation, and pausing. Here's what the authors found:

- More-fluent readers (measured by speed and accuracy) read with better prosody than less-fluent readers.

- Prosody predicted students' comprehension skills above and beyond rate and accuracy for difficult texts but not easy texts. The authors concluded that "reading fluency skill and reading prosody taken together provide a better indicator of reading comprehension than either skill alone" (Benjamin and Schwanenflugel 2010, 399). This relationship held true for both skilled and less skilled readers. The authors noted, "Our less skilled readers, despite making more intrasentential pauses, tended to try to synchronize those pauses with grammatically relevant places in the text in their reading of complex texts. This suggests that even less skilled readers were attempting to use their prosody to support the processing of the difficult texts" (401). We find it fascinating that even less-fluent readers, who paused more when reading, partly because of decoding issues, still attempted to match their pausing to grammatically relevant places in the difficult text.

This prosody study aligns with the Active View of Reading, which holds that prosody may be a bridge between automatic word recognition and comprehension specifically for difficult texts (Duke and Cartwright 2021). Students, regardless of fluency ability, seemed to use prosody as a self-support mechanism when reading the more difficult text.

So how does it work? We know that automatic, accurate word recognition is related to comprehension. When decoding is automatic and relatively effortless, the reader can use those finite cognitive resources to enhance comprehension. Benjamin and Schwanenflugel concluded:

> Children with good comprehension skills had more exaggerated prosody in general. We would argue that these cognitive resources that are freed up from having quick and accurate reading seem to be actively recruited to amplify reading prosody particularly for the purpose of enhancing the comprehension

> of complex text. We believe that complex text is more likely to encourage the use of good reading prosody, because children need it for comprehension. (2010, 401)

Automaticity and accuracy of word recognition free up mental resources for prosody, which readers use to chunk texts into meaningful units in ways that can be used to ease the mental load associated with reading difficult texts. If readers lean on prosody to ease the cognitive load associated with comprehension, it makes sense that this relationship is strongest with difficult text. And that is just what the authors found. Prosody was related to comprehension of difficult but not easier texts!

So What? Actions for the Classroom

Assess Oral Reading Fluency and Comprehension with Texts That Are Above Students' Current Reading Level

You are more likely to hear students employ their prosody abilities with difficult texts. Measuring prosody with a difficult text provides a better window into students' general fluency abilities. Even less-fluent readers can practice prosody with difficult texts. Additionally, prosody with difficult text predicts reading comprehension beyond simple measures of reading rate. However, remember that fluency is necessary but not sufficient for comprehension. Fluency measures (including prosody) "only accounted for approximately 60 percent of the variance in reading skill" (Benjamin and Schwanenflugel 2010, 402).

Differentiate Texts by Difficulty Level for Fluency Practice in Small-Group Instruction

Your stronger readers need challenging texts to continue improving their prosody! If they are reading grade-level text independently, it may be time to increase the level of text difficulty in small-group instruction.

Measure Students' Prosody with Multiple Measures, and Track Text Difficulty

Measuring students' prosody with spectrograms is simply not practical or achievable for the classroom. Therefore, if you're measuring students' prosody, we recommend using measures that go beyond single variables that combine elements of prosody. Similarly, Benjamin and Schwanenflugel recommend that when tracking students' prosody, be sure to indicate the text difficulty and supplement with measures of reading rate and accuracy. We recommend using the Multidimensional Fluency Scale (Figure 12.1), which separates fluency into four criteria: expression and volume, phrasing, smoothness, and pace.

Figure 12.1 Multidimensional Fluency Scale

	1	2	3	4
Expression and Volume	Reads in a quiet voice as if to get words out. The reading does not sound natural like talking to a friend.	Reads in a quiet voice. The reading sounds natural in part of the text, but the reader does not always sound like they are talking to a friend.	Reads with volume and expression. However, sometimes the reader slips into expressionless reading and does not sound like they are talking to a friend.	Reads with varied volume and expression. The reader sounds like they are talking to a friend, with their voice matching the interpretation of the passage.
Phrasing	Reads word-by-word in a monotone voice.	Reads in two- or three-word phrases, not adhering to punctuation, stress, and intonation.	Reads with a mixture of run-ons, mid-sentence pauses for breath, and some choppiness. There is reasonable stress and intonation.	Reads with good phrasing; adhering to punctuation, stress, and intonation.
Smoothness	Frequently hesitates while reading, sounds out words, and repeats words or phrases. The reader makes multiple attempts to read the same passage.	Reads with extended pauses or hesitations. The reader has many "rough spots."	Reads with occasional breaks in rhythm. The reader has difficulty with specific words and/or sentence structures.	Reads smoothly with some breaks, but self-corrects with difficult words and/or sentence structures.
Pace	Reads slowly and laboriously.	Reads moderately slowly.	Reads fast and slow throughout the text.	Reads at a conversational pace throughout the text.

Source: Adapted from Jerry Zutell and Timothy J. Rasinski, "Training Teachers to Attend to Their Students' Oral Reading Fluency." *Theory into Practice*, Vol. 30., 1991.

Caveats and Cautions

→ This study did not address the ideal range of text difficulty for readers. Question 20 provides additional information about the limits of stretch or text difficulty when it comes to reading comprehension. This topic continues to be an evolving area of research.

→ This study focused on second graders and did not address students with reading-specific learning disabilities. As educators, we need to be careful of generalizing the results to all elementary students.

→ This study was not an instructional intervention study. Further research is needed to confirm the long-term benefits of orally reading challenging texts.

What types of texts should we use when working on reading with expression?

TRY THIS — STRETCH

AVOID — INDEPENDENT

Key Findings in Second Grade:
- When assessing prosody, reading more difficult texts led to better prosody for all students, across fluency levels.
- Prosody predicted comprehension above rate and accuracy.

Actions for the Classroom
- Practice oral reading of texts above students' current reading level.
- Differentiate texts by difficulty level in small groups.
- Even less-fluent readers can practice prosody with difficult text.
- Use multiple measures to track students' prosody.

(Benjamin and Schwanenflugel 2010)

Other Useful Resources

Duke, N. K., and K. B. Cartwright. 2021. "The Science of Reading Progresses: Communicating Advances Beyond the Simple View of Reading." *Reading Research Quarterly* 56 (S1): S25–S44.

Grote-Garcia, S., and E. Ortlieb. 2023. "What's Hot in Literacy: The Duality of Explicit Instruction and Cultural and Linguistic Considerations." *Literacy Research and Instruction* 62 (1): 1–15.

Kuhn, M. R., P. J. Schwanenflugel, E. B. Meisinger, B. A. Levy, and T. V. Rasinski, eds. 2010. "Aligning Theory and Assessment of Reading Fluency: Automaticity, Prosody, and Definitions of Fluency." *Reading Research Quarterly* 45 (2): 230–251.

National Institute of Child Health and Human Development, National Institute of Health, and Department of Health and Human Services (NICHD). 2000. *Report of the National Reading Panel: Teaching Children to Read: Reports of the Subgroups* (00-4754). U.S. Government Printing Office.

Schwanenflugel, P. J., A. M. Hamilton, J. M. Wisenbaker, M. R. Kuhn, and S. A. Stahl. 2004. "Becoming a Fluent Reader: Reading Skill and Prosodic Features in the Oral Reading of Young Readers." *Journal of Educational Psychology* 96 (1): 119–129.

Young, C., D. Paige, and T. V. Rasinski. 2022. *Artfully Teaching the Science of Reading*. New York: Routledge.

Zutell, J., and T. V. Rasinski. 1991. "Training Teachers to Attend to Their Students' Oral Reading Fluency." *Theory into Practice* 30 (3): 211–217.

Question 13

What are key components of effective instructional routines for vocabulary?

Discussion from the Classroom

Our work involves preparing educators who are studying to become reading specialists. In a recent discussion of schoolwide reform, one teacher brought her school's data, which included scores that highlighted a low vocabulary and comprehension trend across grade levels. She wondered the following: "I know that vocabulary knowledge is a major predictor of students' comprehension. How do we increase students' vocabulary across grade levels? What would it take to move the needle? And how long would this work take?" While most teachers recognize the important role vocabulary plays on students' comprehension, most vocabulary questions that we field from teachers are localized or related to improving vocabulary and comprehension of a particular text. This teacher's perceptive question and desire for a schoolwide plan points to the role that generalized vocabulary knowledge plays in reading comprehension at large.

Background and Assumptions

Vocabulary knowledge is positively associated with various measures of reading achievement, such as reading comprehension, writing, and content learning. We also know that explicitly pre-teaching vocabulary words leads to better comprehension of texts that include those words (e.g., Wright and Cervetti 2017). However, what is less clear is how teachers can accelerate the overall volume of students' vocabulary knowledge.

Recently, researchers have conducted meta-analyses to compare the effects of word-meaning instruction, where teachers explicitly introduce new vocabulary words, with word-learning strategy instruction that includes teaching students how to infer meaning from external context clues and internal word parts or affixes and roots.

Research Studies That Inform the Question

Cervetti, G. N., M. S. Fitzgerald, E. Hiebert, and M. Hebert. 2023. "Meta-Analysis Examining the Impact of Vocabulary Instruction on Vocabulary Knowledge and Skill." *Reading Psychology* 44 (6): 672–709.

Ellerman, A. M., E. J. Lindo, P. Morphy, and D. L. Compton. 2009. "The Impact of Vocabulary Instruction on Passage-Level Comprehension of School-Age Children: A Meta-Analysis." *Journal of Research on Educational Effectiveness* 2 (1): 1–44.

Manyak, P., L. Z. Blachowicz, and M. Graves. 2021. "The Multifaceted, Comprehensive Vocabulary Instructional Program: Quantitative Findings from a Three-Year Formative Experiment." *Literacy Research and Instruction* 60 (4): 301–331.

Manyak, P. C., and A.-M. Manyak. 2021. "Multi-Faceted Vocabulary Instruction in a Third-Grade Class: Findings from a Three-Year Formative Experiment." *Reading Psychology* 42 (2): 73–110.

Research Findings

Direct Vocabulary Instruction Is Necessary but Not Sufficient for Growing Students' General Vocabulary Knowledge

Pre-teaching key vocabulary words by providing student-friendly definitions with examples and non-examples is a ubiquitous teaching practice in literacy instruction. Pre-teaching vocabulary before reading builds students' prior knowledge of unfamiliar concepts. However, according to a meta-analysis of vocabulary instruction, explicitly teaching vocabulary terms is not enough. By itself, direct instruction of vocabulary did not result in growing students' overall breadth of vocabulary knowledge (Cervetti et al. 2023). At first, this finding struck us as surprising, since the average length of the vocabulary-meaning intervention lasted twenty-three hours in one meta-analysis (Cervetti et al. 2023). However, when typical students learn upwards of two to three thousand words a year (Anderson and Nagy 1992), your vocabulary instruction cannot solely rely on pre-teaching a handful of words each week. Think about it: even if you explicitly taught ten words a week, that would only add up to 10 to 20 percent of the words students learn in a year! Instead, we encourage teachers to think of direct instruction of key vocabulary as a necessary but not sufficient component of their vocabulary instruction. Students will learn the vocabulary they are taught, and this will help them comprehend the texts they are reading that contain those pre-taught words (as measured by custom measures, see Ellerman et al. 2009). However, the direct instruction of core vocabulary terms by itself is not enough.

Teaching Vocabulary Is Especially Important for Students with Reading Difficulties

Ellerman and colleagues found that students with reading difficulties made more than three times the gains in reading comprehension as a result of the vocabulary interventions when compared to typical readers (2009). (The effect size was .39 for typical readers and 1.23 for students with reading difficulties). This makes sense—students with reading difficulties may rely heavily on teacher-directed vocabulary instruction to grow their vocabulary of words that may not otherwise be accessible. The authors also posited that making unknown vocabulary words accessible for students with reading difficulties may free up cognitive resources needed for sophisticated comprehension.

Word-Learning Strategies Have Positive, but Limited, Impact on General Vocabulary Knowledge

Not surprisingly, students who learn word-learning strategies, such as context clues, word parts, or morphemes, improve their abilities to solve unknown words (Cervetti et al. 2023; Ellerman et al. 2009). However, similar to vocabulary-meaning strategies, word-learning strategies had positive effects on custom measures of comprehension but not on generalized measures of vocabulary or comprehension (Ellerman et al. 2009). At first, these findings appear at odds with one another. Students become better at figuring out the meanings of unknown words, but this does not translate to improved scores on generalized vocabulary. Cervetti and fellow authors concluded, "Elementary students may need ongoing opportunities and instructional support over extended periods of times (e.g., several months, multiple school years) to consistently and successfully apply word-solving skills in their reading in order to increase vocabulary knowledge" (2023, 29). They noted that the word-learning strategies interventions they studied typically lasted only sixteen hours, 40 percent less than the typical word-meaning interventions.

Effective Vocabulary Instruction Is Multi-Faceted

There appears to be no one magic bullet that will significantly improve students' overall vocabulary. However, it turns out that multi-component, sustained vocabulary instruction can potentially lead to larger-than-expected gains in generalized vocabulary.

Manyak, Blachowicz, and Graves (2021) conducted a three-year formative experiment with thirty fourth and fifth grade classrooms across three regions. In their Multifaceted Comprehensive Vocabulary Instruction Program (MCVIP), students experienced daily focused vocabulary instruction in their language arts block, which included regular review activities. Explicit instruction of "key target word meanings" was also integrated into content-area instruction. The vocabulary program included four elements: (a) providing rich and varied language experiences; (b) teaching individual words; (c) teaching word-learning strategies, including morphology; and (d) fostering word consciousness.

Students' vocabulary was measured at the beginning and end of the year using both custom research-created measures and a standardized measure of vocabulary growth (words were not pre-taught). (Research-created measures included assessment of students' learning of explicitly taught words, morphemic analysis, and ability to use context clues to infer word meanings. The standardized assessment was the Gates-MacGinitie Reading Tests Vocabulary Subtests, 4th edition.) Students in both grades, regardless of school, made significant growth in all of the researcher-created measures. More significantly, by Year 3 of the study, the researchers noted that students who received MCVIP instruction "made 1.3 and 1.5 years of growth in general vocabulary knowledge during the course of one academic year" (Manyak, Blachowicz, and Graves 2021, 319).

Group Size May Not Matter, But Discussion Does

The meta-analysis conducted by Ellerman et al. (2009) examined the impact of several characteristics of instruction. Interestingly, they found that group size for vocabulary instruction did not matter. Small groups were not more effective than whole-group instruction when compared across K–12 classrooms. They also found that the use of high levels of student discussion was associated with greater effects on research-created vocabulary measures (e.g., of targeted vocabulary).

So What? Actions for the Classroom

Include Immediate and Long-Term Vocabulary Instruction

Students understand text better when teachers have explicitly pre-taught unfamiliar vocabulary words. When students tackle a new text in small-group instruction or as a read-aloud, teachers should strategically identify those words that will help them comprehend the text. While teaching individual words explicitly is key to building students' comprehension of the present text or even a thematic unit, it is not sufficient by itself to accelerate students' vocabulary growth and improve general reading comprehension. Instead, robust vocabulary instruction that has multiple components, including word-learning strategies, is needed. Vocabulary instruction must go beyond thinking about the demands of the present text and include multi-faceted, long-term vocabulary routines and instruction. In addition to teaching individual words, this robust instruction should include rich oral-language opportunities, such as those found in interactive read-alouds, and flooding students with a wide range of diverse words and then providing them with opportunities to apply those words. For example, students may collectively curate and display images that illustrate new terms learned in the content areas on a digital platform or even a classroom word wall (Manyak, Manyak, and Kappus 2021). See Figure 13.2 for an example of a weekly schedule that includes approximately twenty-five minutes daily dedicated to vocabulary instruction.

Explicitly Teach Target Words Related to Texts

Teaching individual words and word-learning strategies positively impacts students' vocabulary and reading comprehension of focal texts. Explicit instruction should include a brief kid-friendly definition. Before students interact with the word, the teacher should provide examples and non-examples of the word. The teacher can do this by showing pictures and acting out the word. We encourage teachers to discuss the word within the context of the text and also provide relatable examples to students' lives. Students should then be given opportunities to work with the word. Sentence stems for student-provided examples and simple "thumbs up/thumbs down" activities are quick but require student application and ownership of the word. We recommend the National Center for Improving Literacy website (see Other Useful Resources on page 122) for a helpful infographic and routine that outlines these steps. Figure 13.2 outlines a brief, four-step routine for explicitly introducing vocabulary.

Develop Word-Learning Strategies

Vocabulary instruction must also include teaching students strategies for feeding their own developing vocabulary knowledge when they are reading independently. This incidental learning accounts for the vast vocabulary gains that readers make each year. One important way we support students as independent word learners is by building their morphemic knowledge of word parts (prefixes, suffixes, and Greek and Latin roots). Teaching routines or processes to read longer words can be beneficial, especially when the steps involve recognizing root words and prefixes and suffixes (see Kearns and Whaley 2019 for a review of strategies). Figure 13.1 includes an example of how students might decode a longer, multisyllabic word while also building word knowledge through affixes. We adapted the Peeling Off technique by adding steps that call students' attention to word meaning (Lovett et al. 2000 and Lovett et al. 2017 as cited by Kearns and Whaley 2019). The ESHALOV technique is a syllable-based strategy based on the "Every syllable has at least one vowel" principle (O'Connor et al. 2015).

Figure 13.1. Example of the Adapted Peeling Off and ESHALOV Techniques for Decoding and Determining Word Meaning for Longer Words

Mis·un·der·stand·ing

Adapted Peeling Off Technique

1. Circle the prefixes and suffixes.
2. Say the prefixes and suffixes.
3. Check meaning of prefixes and suffixes.
4. Say the root.
5. Say the whole word
6. Check the meaning of the whole word by reading the sentence.

To decode a multisyllabic root, students may use the ESHALOV method to break the root into syllables. "Each syllable has at least one vowel." Here, the root is underlined and dots are used to indicate possible syllable breaks.

Source: The Peeling Off and ESHALOV techniques are described in Kearns and Whaley (2019). The Peeling Off technique was modified to include word meaning.

Notice, however, that these routines require a base level of knowledge about the meanings of these morphemes, or word parts. Just as we must explicitly teach individual words, we also want to explicitly teach common morphemes. In addition to morphemic analysis, another word-learning strategy is teaching students how to infer the meaning of unfamiliar words from context clues.

Cautions and Caveats

→ Additional research is needed to study the impacts of multi-component and longer-term vocabulary instruction. Most research on vocabulary interventions is short term. In Ellerman's research, over half of the studies lasted ten hours or fewer. Only a few studies have lasted an entire school year.

→ MCVIP, which is one of the few interventions to show generalized vocabulary growth, is a yearlong program, with some students experiencing two years of daily instruction (Manyak, Blachowicz, and Graves 2021). This study compared MCVIP students' growth to nationally normed expectations of growth. In other words, there was not a control group for this study, and students' comprehension was not measured as part of the research. Additional research is needed to support schools' and districts' efforts at spiraling and supporting students' vocabulary acquisition across grade levels.

Figure 13.2 Example of Explicit Instruction During a Fourth Grade Read-Aloud of *After the Fall* by Dan Santat

Components to Explicit Vocabulary Instruction	Sample Teacher Language
Student-Friendly Definitions	• We learned a new word related to our character today. Humpty Dumpty in our book showed <u>persistence</u>. Persistence is when someone keeps trying even when it is hard or they experience failure. • We would describe a character as <u>persistent</u> if they keep trying even when it is really hard.
Examples and Non-Examples	• In our book, Humpty Dumpty showed <u>persistence</u> when he kept trying to build a paper airplane over and over again. He got paper cuts and he was frustrated, but he never gave up! Humpty Dumpty is persistent! • If I try a math problem and I give up after one minute, I'm not showing <u>persistence</u>. • Last week, we read a book about Michael Jordan, the famous basketball player. He practiced every day when he was a kid. He never stopped trying to improve. He was <u>persistent</u>. • The fifth grader was <u>persistent</u> when trying to convince his parents to get him a phone. He left notes around the house. He asked them every day. He did chores to earn money.
Visual Images	• This illustration shows Humpty Dumpty trying to make the perfect airplane. How is Dan Santat, the illustrator, showing you that Humpty Dumpty is <u>persistent</u>? • Here is a picture of a woman hiking up a steep mountain. How is she showing <u>persistence</u>?
Student Application	• Tell your partner about a time when you were <u>persistent</u>. You can start your sentence like this, "I was persistent when . . ." • Give me a thumbs up or thumbs down if a character showed <u>persistence</u>. • Tell your partner about a TV or book character who was <u>persistent</u>. "*Blank* was persistent when . . ." • We are learning about Jackie Robinson in history. Who can explain how Jackie Robinson was <u>persistent</u>? • Many of you are writing biographies of famous Americans who showed persistence. Today, when you are writing, consider writing about how your person demonstrated <u>persistence</u>.

What are key components of effective instructional routines for vocabulary?

Sample Weekly Routine

	MONDAY	**TUESDAY**	**WEDNESDAY**
Effective Practice	Explicit instruction of high-utility words	Word-learning strategy practice Review activity of previously learned words	Explicit instruction of high-utility words Connect to writing
Looks Like	From read-aloud of *After the Fall* • "Humpty Dumpty in our book showed persistence. Persistence is when someone keeps trying even when it is hard or they experience failure." • "If I try a math problem and I give up after one minute, I'm not showing persistence." • "This illustration shows Humpty Dumpty trying to make the perfect airplane. How is the illustrator showing you that Humpty Dumpty is persistent?" • "Tell your partner about a time when you were persistent. You can start your sentence with, 'I was persistent when…'"	• Students explore derivations of the root word *persist*: *persistence, persistent*. • Students practice taking apart and reassembling "long" words according to the "root" prefixes and suffixes. • Students play Connect 2, a review game where students share two previously learned words that are connected. Teacher calls on students to explain their connection.	• "We've been talking this week about the theme of persistence. In social studies, many of you are writing biographies of famous people who persisted. Today, when you are writing, consider writing about how your person demonstrated persistence."

Sample Weekly Routine

	THURSDAY	**FRIDAY**	
Effective Practice	Word learning strategy practice Review activity of previously learned words	Word consciousness lesson Character Trait vocabulary lesson	
Looks Like	Students collect and sort "root" prefix words in their vocabulary journals. Students research online to add pictures to their shared Padlet on simple machines. Students play Mind Reader, a review game. Students select a word and write three clues to help others guess it. Students read their clues and others guess.	• Students map their character's traits from small groups onto a digital semantic feature map. Teacher contrasts new traits: decisive and indecisive.	**Effective Vocabulary Routines:** • Embed key target words across content areas. • Include immediate explicit instruction and long-term word learning strategies. • Include regular review and ongoing opportunities to practice. • Empower students as word learners!

(Manyak, Manyak, and Kappus 2021; Manyak et al. 2021)

Other Useful Resources

Anderson, R. C., and W. E. Nagy. 1992. "The Vocabulary Conundrum." *American Educator* 16 (4): 14–18, 44–47.

Kearns, D. M., and V. M. Whaley. 2019. "Helping Students with Dyslexia Read Long Words: Using Syllables and Morphemes." *Teaching Exceptional Children* 51 (3): 212–225.

Lovett, M. W., J. C. Frijters, M. Wolf, K. A. Steinbach, R. A. Sevcik, and R. D. Morris. 2017. "Early Intervention for Children at Risk for Reading Disabilities: The Impact of Grade at Intervention and Individual Differences on Intervention Outcomes." *Journal of Educational Psychology* 109 (7): 889–914.

Lovett, M. W., L. Lacerenza, S. L. Borden, J. C. Frijters, K. A. Steinbach, and M. De Palma. 2000. "Components of Effective Remediation for Developmental Reading Disabilities: Combining Phonological and Strategy-Based Instruction to Improve Outcomes." *Journal of Educational Psychology* 92 (2): 263–283.

Manyak, P. C., A.-M. Manyak, and E. M. Kappus. 2021. "Lessons from a Decade of Research on Multifaceted Vocabulary Instruction." *The Reading Teacher* 75 (1): 27–39.

National Center on Improving Literacy. 2023. *The Educator's Science of Reading Toolbox: Explicit Vocabulary Instruction to Build Equitable Access for All Learners.* Washington, DC: U.S. Department of Education, Office of Elementary and Secondary Education, Office of Special Education Programs, National Center on Improving Literacy. improvingliteracy.org/code-assets/briefs/explicit-vocabulary-instruction.pdf.

O'Connor, R. E., K. D. Beach, V. M. Sanchez, K. M. Bocian, and L. J. Flynn. 2015. "Building BRIDGES: A Design Experiment to Improve Reading and United States History Knowledge of Poor Readers in Eighth Grade." *Exceptional Children* 81 (4) 399–425.

Wright, T. S., and G. N. Cervetti. 2017. "A Systematic Review of the Research on Vocabulary Instruction That Impacts Text Comprehension." *Reading Research Quarterly* 52 (2): 203–226.

Question 14

Should I teach comprehension strategies one at a time by week?

Discussion from the Classroom

In a typical third to fifth grade classroom where the teacher provides primarily whole-class instruction using a core basal reading program, an observer might expect to see a sequence similar to the following:

→ On Monday, the teacher introduces Gail Gibbons's book *Alligators and Crocodiles* (2010), introduces and discusses new vocabulary, and activates students' prior knowledge about what animals eat, where they live, and their characteristics. She then introduces the compare-and-contrast text structure and models what it looks like in the week's selected text.

→ From Tuesday to Thursday, the students learn cue words and phrases such as *similar, unlike, although, on the other hand,* and *likewise,* and apply them to the text. They also answer teacher-provided questions related to the text. They then practice writing a paragraph comparing alligators and crocodiles using a paragraph frame. During the week, they independently read and research for their animal reports, where they are expected to have a page layout that applies the compare-and-contrast text structure.

→ In the week that follows, the same cycle is repeated with a new text structure and story. It may be several weeks until students transition into a new strategy or are prompted to apply previously learned strategies.

Almasi and Hart (2019) characterize this type of instruction as focusing on teaching *strategies*, instead of teaching students to be *strategic,* which involves empowering students to intentionally employ strategies when they encounter difficulties when reading. The latter type of instruction develops metacognitive readers who know when and how to use the strategies flexibly, which is ultimately the goal of comprehension instruction.

Comprehension strategies are research based. We've known for decades that good adult readers flexibly apply and adapt comprehension strategies while actively processing text (Pressley and Afflerbach 1995). We also know from research that teachers can effectively teach these individual strategies, text structures included, to their students. While we can all agree that the end goal is for our students to flexibly use a repertoire of strategies, we have not always agreed on how to get them to this end goal. Teachers have typically taken two different approaches, a single-strategy approach versus a multiple-strategies approach.

Background and Assumptions

Professional learning resources on the topic of strategy instruction have traditionally focused on the benefits of teaching individual strategies to students in isolation. Comprehension research in the 1980s and '90s also focused on the impact of teaching individual strategies to students. Many professional education books have chapters dedicated to teaching individual strategies, following the one-strategy approach where the teacher introduces a strategy with direct instruction and modeling. The teacher then provides extensive, scaffolded support in the form of anchor charts and graphic organizers and opportunities for student practice that sometimes occur over weeks (*Mosaic of Thought* and *Strategies at Work* are two popular examples that come to mind).

A contrasting approach involves quickly introducing a core group of strategies through direct instruction and modeling and then providing guided practice and coaching around integrating the strategies with different texts. Such multi-strategy approaches include Reciprocal Teaching (Palincsar and Brown 1984), Transactional Strategies Instruction (Brown et al. 1996), Learning Strategies Curriculum (Cantrell et al. 2016), and Collaborative Strategic Reading (Klingner et al. 2004). These multi-strategy approaches consistently and positively impact students' reading comprehension across age and ability levels. In the multiple-strategies approach, student conversations (with teacher guidance) around integrated strategy use are foregrounded. Some approaches, such as Reciprocal Teaching, provide more structure to these conversations, where students take on strategy roles and strategy use occurs in more of a stepped fashion. In other approaches, such as Transactional Strategies Instruction, the meaning of the text is co-constructed by the group as they discuss the text and use the strategies to solve breakdowns or snags in comprehension (Pressley and El-Dinary 1997; Brown et al. 1996).

Research Studies That Inform the Question

Brown, R., M. Pressley, P. Van Meter, and T. Schuder. 1996. "A Quasi-Experimental Validation of Transactional Strategies Instruction with Low-Achieving Second-Grade Readers." *Journal of Educational Psychology* **88 (1): 18–37.**

Reutzel, D. R., J. A. Smith, and P. C. Fawson. 2005. "An Evaluation of Two Approaches for Teaching Reading Comprehension Strategies in the Primary Years Using Science Information Texts." *Early Childhood Research Quarterly* **20 (3): 276–305.**

Research Findings

Transactional Strategies Instruction (TSI) is one multi-strategy instructional approach. The purpose of TSI is to create readers who are active problem-solvers who monitor their comprehension as they read. As part of this process, students are taught to activate their background knowledge and apply a range of strategies to achieve these goals. Brown, Pressley, Van Meter, and Schuder (1996) conducted an experimental study involving sixty second graders who were reading below grade level at the beginning of the year. At the end of the year, students in the multiple strategies classrooms reported using more comprehension and word-solving strategies.

In another study involving second graders, researchers investigated a semester-long project with four classrooms from a low-performing, high-poverty school where over 50 percent of students received free or reduced lunch (Reutzel, Smith, and Fawson 2005). Teachers and students were randomly assigned to two conditions: (a) single-strategy instruction in isolation and (b) multi-strategies instruction that focused on informational science content and texts.

In the single-strategy condition, teachers taught a total of six comprehension strategies, one at a time. Students received instruction and practiced a single strategy during a thirteen-day instructional cycle. During the strategy cycle, teachers spent five days modeling the strategy with one informational big book focusing on science content. The teachers then engaged students in interactive discussions during additional read-alouds for the next five to six days. Each instructional cycle wrapped up with small groups and independent practice.

In the multiple-strategies condition, each of the eight comprehension strategies were originally introduced and modeled during three days over a week (80–120 minutes) with a single informational science big book. This cycle was repeated over the course of the first month. During the second and third months, the teachers modeled integrating strategies, and students practiced selecting, explaining, and integrating all eight strategies while reading the remaining books.

Reutzel, Smith, and Fawson (2005) found no significant differences in measures of standardized comprehension outcomes (Gates-MacGinitie Reading Test) or motivation across the two conditions. However, the multi-strategies condition was associated with statistically higher scores on recall and science content-knowledge acquisition. Furthermore, scores on the state curriculum-based comprehension test demonstrated a significant advantage for the multi-strategies condition.

These two studies serve as important reminders that teaching students how to flexibly use a group of reading-comprehension strategies can lead to significant improvements in students' comprehension of informational text as early as second grade. Furthermore, they suggest that comprehension instruction should focus more on strategic thinking and go beyond merely teaching individual strategies in isolation (Almasi and Hart 2019).

So What? Actions for the Classroom

Students Need Opportunities to Integrate Strategies

When reading about multiple-strategies instruction in the literature, the metaphor of the teacher "orchestrating" dynamic, in-the-moment, student-focused conversations is often used. This orchestration is by its very nature complex. Much like conductors who spend years honing their craft before leading an orchestra, it takes teachers significant time to master this type of complex, high-intensity teaching (Pressley and El-Dinary 1997), which may be part of the reason Stahl (2004) classified it as "having a strong research base in the primary grades" but of "limited use by teachers" (599).

So, while this dynamic, multiple-strategies instruction is possible and leads to positive growth, it may not always be practical or doable, especially for new teachers or teachers transitioning grades. District reading coaches may also have legitimate questions about the scalability of this approach across grade levels when programs like TSI are more fluid and less structured or scripted. From our years of practical work in classrooms, we have noticed that many teachers, especially those in the primary grades, may initially be more comfortable applying a single-strategy approach where they introduce individual strategies one at a time. They make sure to teach the declarative (what the strategy is), procedural (how to use it), and conditional (when it is most helpful) strategy knowledge associated with the single strategy before adding a new one. However, by itself, this single-strategy approach is incomplete and may not lead to the type of strategic thinking recommended by Almasi and Hart (2019). When introducing individual strategies, it is critical that teachers include ongoing modeling and student practice integrating the newly mastered strategy into their growing repertoire of strategies. For example, as students practice the summarizing strategy while reading a new informational text, they are still stopping to ask and answer questions (a previously learned strategy), and they have opportunities to practice this integration with their peers through small-group discussions.

Embed Conditional-Knowledge Instruction and Small-Group Discussions into Basal Programs

We also note that integrated multiple-strategies instruction appears historically absent in many basal programs (Dewitz, Jones, and Leahy 2009). If your district's scope and sequence incorporates a core basal program, be sure to make time in the schedule for small-group discussions where students practice integrating a newly learned strategy with previously learned strategies. Also, be sure to include instruction on when and how to use the strategies.

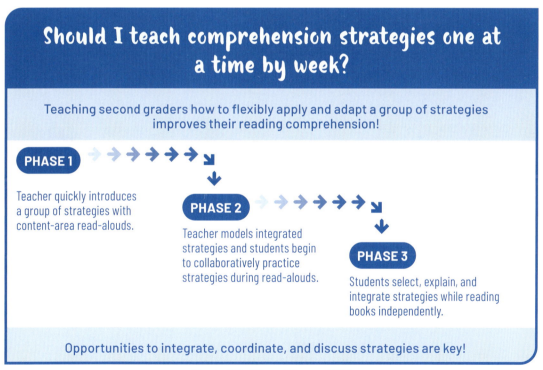

(Reutzel, Smith, and Fawson 2005)

Cautions and Caveats

As with much of the comprehension intervention research, the studies summarized here did not result in significant gains on standardized reading comprehension tests. We also caution that additional research comparing the single- to multiple-strategies approaches is needed to confirm Reutzel and colleagues' findings, as that study involved only four second grade classrooms.

Other Useful Resources

Almasi, J. F., and S. J. Hart. 2019. "Best Practices in Narrative Text Comprehension Instruction." In *Best Practices in Literacy Instruction* **(6th ed.), edited by L. M. Morrow and L. Gambrell, 221–249. New York: Guilford Press.**

Dewitz, P., J. Jones, and S. Leahy. 2009. "Comprehension Strategy Instruction in Core Reading Programs." *Reading Research Quarterly* **44 (2): 102–126.**

Pressley, M., and P. B. El-Dinary. 1997. "What We Know About Translating Comprehension Strategies Instruction Research into Practice." *Journal of Learning Disabilities* **30 (5): 486–488.**

Stahl, K. 2004. "Proof, Practice, and Promise: Comprehension Strategy Instruction in the Primary Grades." *The Reading Teacher* **57 (7): 598–609.**

Question 15

Which comprehension strategies are most important to teach, and how many should I teach? Are there certain groups or combinations of strategies that work best?

Discussion from the Classroom

A literacy coach for a district recently emailed one of us. She is working with her team of school-based reading specialists to revise their curriculum scope and sequence for comprehension for fourth and fifth grades. The coach shared that the teachers are debating which and how many reading-comprehension strategies should be included in the scope and sequence. She noted that their school has a high percentage of students who are reading significantly below grade level in fourth grade. The teachers have been working with students in small groups on building students' decoding skills. The coach shared the teachers' frustration that teaching multi-strategies is complex. Many of them wondered, "Which ones should I focus on, and how many are 'enough'?"

Background and Assumptions

Activating and building students' prior knowledge of texts before reading helps students by reducing the cognitive load involved in reading complex texts (Willingham 2006). It is believed that strong prior knowledge allows students to combine information in their short-term memory and then easily transfer new information to their long-term memory. Thus, activating their prior knowledge frees up working memory space, which is especially helpful for students who struggle with reading or who have a reading disability (Filderman et al. 2022). Similarly, reading-comprehension strategies "can help readers stay engaged and efficiently use the limited cognitive resources to organize information during reading comprehension" (Peng et al. 2023, 230).

Research Studies That Inform the Question

Filderman, M. J., C. R. Austin, A. N., Boucher, K. O'Donnell, and E. A. Swanson. 2022. "A Meta-Analysis of the Effects of Reading Comprehension Interventions on the Reading Comprehension Outcomes of Struggling Readers in Third through 12th Grades." *Exceptional Children* 88 (2): 163–184.

Peng, P., W. Wang, M. J. Filderman, W. Zhang, and L. Lin. 2023. "The Active Ingredient in Reading Comprehension Strategy Intervention for Struggling Readers: A Bayeseian Network Meta-Analysis." *Review of Educational Research* 94 (2): 228–267.

Research Findings

A recent meta-analysis included fifty-two studies that investigated the impact that different comprehension-strategy combinations had on struggling readers' comprehension in grades 3–12 (Peng et al. 2023). The meta-analysis included the following strategies:

- main idea
- inference
- text structure
- retell, prediction
- self-monitoring
- graphic organizers

Piling on More Strategies Is Not Necessarily Better

The authors found that "instruction of more strategies did not necessarily have stronger effects on reading comprehension" (Peng et al. 2023, 1). Rather, the three most effective combinations of strategies contained no more than four strategies and all involved teaching the main idea. The authors noted "that many strategy combinations that included three or more strategies did not necessarily produce bigger effects than strategy combinations with a smaller number of strategies. We even noticed some five- or six-strategy combinations showed smaller effects on reading comprehension than a single strategy intervention or intervention with fewer strategies instruction" (24). Thus,

Peng and colleagues found no correlation between the number of strategies and the effect size of reading comprehension but suggest that teaching the main idea may be a key strategy to teach to students with reading difficulties.

Activating or Building Background Knowledge Works Synergistically When Paired with Other Comprehension Strategies

There appears to be an "ingredient interaction" in comprehension instruction, which means the effects of reading comprehension–strategy instruction are biggest when combined with background knowledge (Peng et al. 2023). The authors stated that "the effects of strategies only held when background knowledge instruction was included" (1). This finding is consistent with another meta-analysis that found that including background knowledge as part of an intervention significantly predicts the effectiveness of comprehension instruction (Filderman et al. 2022).

So What? Actions for the Classroom

Activate and Build Background Knowledge in Tandem with Comprehension Strategies

Prior knowledge is one of those ubiquitous topics that we all learn about in our teacher preparation programs—and for good reason! Activating and building background knowledge makes learning new information from text a lot easier. There are many ways teachers can do this effectively:

- → First, pair texts together. This can include pairing a nonfiction with a fiction text. For example, you could read a short newspaper article on the 1906 San Francisco earthquake before reading a narrative, fictionalized account to help students get a better understanding of the time line and effects of the earthquake. Many such paired texts are offered for free at Readworks.org.

- → Teach students to preview informational texts, looking for headings, graphics, and boldface terms while thinking about what they already know in relation to these key concepts and terms.

- → Build students' background knowledge by watching and discussing videos, examining photos, and visiting informational websites prior to reading about unfamiliar concepts.

- → To encourage rich discussion, use the Four Corners technique, which involves posting four statements related to a topic around the room. Students then physically move to the statement they agree with the most. Students in each location discuss why they agree with that statement, and then one person from each corner shares out with the whole group. This is a great way to learn from one another prior to and even after reading (Ferlazzo and Sypnieski 2018).

While activating students' prior knowledge of complex text is absolutely necessary, we want to make sure that students are actively monitoring and applying a small set of strategies to comprehend that text. Activating prior knowledge should illuminate, not overshadow, the text.

Cluster-Teach Key Strategies for Mastery

In the meta-analysis described above, Peng and his fellow authors (2023) concluded that the optimal combination of strategies may include the main idea, text structure, and retell combination. They hypothesize that main idea and retelling may work as "umbrella strategies" that incorporate elements of other strategies. However, they noted that there is no "most important" single strategy. On the other hand, teaching a repertoire of five or more strategies may overwhelm the cognitive load for struggling readers. Even if they learn the individual strategies, it may be too much to practice when reading independently.

When we read the results of this study, it reminded us of the decades of research done on Reciprocal Teaching, an instructional practice where students are taught to use just four strategies when reading: predicting, questioning, summarizing, and clarifying (e.g., Palincsar and Brown 1984). The strategies are quickly introduced and modeled by the teacher, and students then gain supported practice using the strategies in small groups as they read texts. It struck us that main idea and retelling are part of the summarizing and clarifying strategies. When students summarize, they are identifying main ideas and supporting details. Part of the purpose of recalling is to clarify or monitor understanding. In Reciprocal Teaching, students are taught to use their background knowledge to make predictions. When we think back to the coach's question that began this exploration, we are left to conclude that activating and building students' prior knowledge is the "secret sauce" to making comprehension strategies effective—and that teaching students a small number of strategies that include main idea and retelling to regularly apply to text would likely work best.

Cautions and Caveats

We have definitely not closed the book when it comes to figuring out which and how many strategies to teach readers of different ages, abilities, and backgrounds and for different texts (e.g., narrative, informational). As noted in Question 14 on comprehension instruction, there is a robust body of research pointing to the efficacy of teaching single strategies (see Filderman et al. 2022 and Gersten, Fuchs, and Baker 2001 for reviews).

There are also decades of research supporting multiple-strategies instruction. However, research in this area continues to evolve, and so we continue to explore research questions about which strategies are necessary, how many are sufficient, and what is the optimal duration of instruction for different groups of readers.

Which comprehension strategies are most important to teach?

Active Ingredient: PRIOR KNOWLEDGE

Cluster Strategies
- There is no single, most-important strategy.
- Piling on more strategies is not necessarily better.
- The optimal strategy combination included main idea, text structure, and retell.

Activate and Build Prior Knowledge
- Use paired texts when planning units.
- Teach students to preview informational texts.
- Build students' background knowledge prior to reading about unfamiliar concepts.

(Filderman et al. 2022; Peng et al. 2023)

Other Useful Resources

Ferlazzo, L., and K. H. Sypnieski. 2018. "Activating Prior Knowledge with English Language Learners." *Edutopia*, March 29, 2018. edutopia.org/article/activating-prior-knowledge-english-language-learners/.

Gersten, R. M., L. Fuchs, and S. K. Baker. 2001. "Teaching Reading Comprehension Strategies to Students with Learning Disabilities: A Review of Research." *Review of Educational Research* 71 (2): 279–320.

Willingham, D. T. 2006. "The Usefulness of Brief Instruction in Reading Comprehension Strategies." *American Educator* 30 (4): 39–50.

Question 16

How can I effectively teach expository text structures, and when should this instruction start?

Discussion from the Classroom

In our work with schools, we find that teachers understand that teaching text structures is important. This general understanding is backed up by over four decades of research. Text structures are how information in texts is organized. There are five primary ways authors organize information when writing expository texts: descriptive, sequential, comparison, cause and effect, and problem and solution (see Roehling et al. 2017 for a summary). It is important to note too that authors often include more than one text structure when writing. Identifying and applying text-structure knowledge to a new expository text helps the reader understand complex texts that are often full of new information and unknown academic vocabulary. In this way, identifying the text structure helps connect and organize important conceptual information in order to recall it in a meaningful way in the future.

However, teacher questions around text structures remain. "How many should I teach at once?" "Which one should I start with?" "How long should I spend on teaching them?" "When should we start this instruction?" Often these questions can be summed up as, "How can I effectively teach expository text structures, and when should this instruction start?"

Background and Assumptions

Figure 16.1 provides a brief, student-friendly description of each of the five main text structures, along with paragraph frames and guiding questions to support instruction.

Figure 16.1. Examples of Paragraph Frames and Guiding Questions for Five Text Structures

Expository Text Structures	Paragraph Frames	Guiding Questions
Descriptive The author shares information and characteristics about something.	A ____ is a type of ____. It is made up of ____ and looks like ____. Some ____ have ____. For example ____.	What is the author describing? What are the details used to describe it?
Sequential The author includes steps, events, or procedures in order.	There are ____ steps in the ____. First, ____. Next, ____. Then, ____. Finally, ____.	What is the first thing that happened? What is the next step? What happened last?
Comparison The author shows how things are alike and different.	____ and ____ are alike in several ways. Both ____ and ____ have similar ____. Both also ____ as well as ____. On the other hand, one way they differ is ____. Another difference is ____ have ____ while ____ have ____.	What objects, concepts, or categories are being compared? How are they the same? How are they different? What features are being compared?
Cause and Effect The author explains why something happened or how something works.	The reason why ____ happened was because of ____. If ____ hadn't happened, then ____. Due to ____ occurring, ____. This explains why ____. The cause of ____ is not easy to define. Some people think the cause is ____. Others believe the main cause is ____. Understanding the cause of ____ is important because ____.	What are the cause(s) and related effect(s)? What happened? Why?
Problem and Solution The author describes a problem and then offers one or more possible solutions.	____ had/is a problem because ____. One possible solution is ____. This answer is good because ____. Therefore, ____. As a result, ____. The problem of ____ really boils down to the issue of ____. In the past, the common solution was to ____. However, this was only effective in terms of ____. There are now other solutions that might work. One option would be to ____.	What were the difficulties or questions? What were the attempts or possible actions to solve them? How was it or might it be solved? What were the consequences of the options? What was the result of the actions?

Sources: Paragraph frames from Robbins and Hilden (2016, 48–50). Guiding questions from Roehling et al. (2017, 74).

Research Studies That Inform the Question

Hebert, M., J. J. Bohaty, J. R. Nelson, and J. Brown. 2016. "The Effects of Text Structure Instruction on Expository Reading Comprehension: A Meta-Analysis." *Journal of Educational Psychology* 108 (5): 609–629.

Pyle, N., A. C. Vasquez, B. Lignugaris/Kraft, S. L. Gillam, D. R. Reutzel, A. Olszewski, H. Segura, D. Hartzheim, W. Laing, and D. Pyle. 2017. "Effects of Expository Text Structure Interventions on Comprehension: A Meta-Analysis." *Reading Research Quarterly* 52 (4): 469–501.

Wijekumar, K., B. J. F. Meyer, P.-W. Lei, A. C. Hernandez, and D. L. August. 2018. "Improving Content Area Reading Comprehension of Spanish Speaking English Learners in Grades 4 and 5 Using Web-Based Text Structure Instruction." *Reading and Writing* 31 (9): 1969-1996.

Williams, J. P., K. M. Hall, K. D. Lauer, K. B. Stafford, L. A. DeSisto, and J. S. deCani. 2005. "Expository Text Comprehension in the Primary Grade Classroom." *Journal of Educational Psychology* 97 (4): 538–550.

Williams, J. P., J. C. Kao, L. S. Pao, J. G. Ordynans, J. G. Atkins, R. Jheng, and D. DeBonis. 2016. "Close Analysis of Texts with Structure (CATS): An Intervention to Teach Reading Comprehension to At-Risk Second Graders." *Journal of Educational Psychology* 108 (8): 1061-1077.

Research Findings

Text-Structure Instruction Is Effective in Elementary Grades for ALL Students

In meta-analysis of twenty-one studies for grades 2–12, text-structure instruction was most effective in the elementary grades (Pyle et al. 2017). A second meta-analysis of forty studies found that text-structure instruction "is equally effective across both elementary and secondary grade levels" (Hebert et al. 2016, 619). Williams' text structure research has consistently demonstrated the positive benefits of teaching expository text structures beginning in second grade (Williams et al. 2005; Williams et al. 2016). This research includes an experimental design where second graders were taught all five expository text structures across fifty social studies lessons. Not only did the students who received text-structure instruction write better summaries, they also learned the content better! The main takeaway here is that text-structure instruction belongs in the elementary grades, as early as second grade.

Text-structure instruction is beneficial for all students regardless of reading ability, including students who have or who are at risk of having a learning disability (Hebert et al. 2016; Pyle et al. 2017).

Wijekumar and colleagues found that text-structure instruction is also effective for multilingual learners (2018). In their study, online instruction for multilingual learners included models of how to apply knowledge of text structures when reading. Students participated in a variety of interactions, such as clicking on signal words, writing main ideas, and answering multiple-choice questions. The online program provided Spanish-language adaptations to support multilingual students. The positive results associated with this study are described below in the section on online instruction.

Duration of Text-Structure Instruction

When it comes to the question of how much time to spend teaching text structures, eleven to twenty hours of instruction seems to be the sweet spot (Pyle et al. 2017). In classrooms where every minute of instruction is precious, it is important to remember that more is not always better in terms of time. What does this look like for teachers? If a teacher were designing a unit focusing on text structures, they would dedicate approximately two hours each week working on this topic. This breaks down to thirty minutes a day, four days a week, for approximately six to ten weeks.

Include Writing When Working on Text Structures

In a meta-analysis, text-structure instruction was more effective when it included writing (Hebert et al. 2016). The types of writing in the reviewed studies included writing sentences, note-taking, and writing paragraphs. Similarly, Graham and Hebert concluded from their meta-analysis that, "Writing about a text proved to be better than just reading it, reading and rereading it, reading and studying it, reading and discussing it, and receiving reading instruction" (2010, 14). This means that text-structure instruction tends to be more effective when it includes students' applying text structures in their expository writing.

Teach More Than One Text Structure

The research on how many text structures to teach is mixed. Pyle and colleagues (2017) found that teaching one or two types of text structures led to larger effects on comprehension measures than teaching three or more. In contrast, other researchers found a small, yet positive effect each time an additional text structure was added (Hebert et al. 2016). The same meta-analysis also found that comprehension of taught structures positively predicted comprehension of untaught structures (Hebert et al. 2016). In a research study with second graders, researchers found that students could successfully apply the comparison text structure to new content; however this specific text-structure instruction did not generalize to text structures that had not been taught (Williams et al. 2005). More research is needed to tease apart the relationships between text structures and how to best spiral this instruction in the elementary grades.

Online Instruction Can Be Effective

In a meta-analysis comparing implementation of text-structure instruction, researcher-provided interventions led to stronger, positive outcomes compared to those taught by teachers or delivered by computer-based tutoring programs (Wijekumar et al. 2018). However, it is noteworthy that online programs that provide individualized text-structure instruction led to small but significant improvement in students' reading comprehension (Pyle et al. 2017). A randomized control study of the online SWELL program suggests potential for future online tutoring programs (Wijekumar et al. 2018). SWELL stands for Strategy Instruction on the Web for English Learners, and it combines text-structure instruction with vocabulary and background knowledge supports. When fourth and fifth grade Spanish-speaking English learners participated in SWELL for forty-five to sixty minutes a week, they significantly outperformed their control counterparts on a standardized test of reading comprehension (Gray Silent Reading Test).

Role of Signal or Clue Words

One common instructional practice includes teaching students to look for signal words that provide clues to the text's structure (Roehling et al. 2017). However, we were surprised to read in a meta-analysis that signal words and explicit instruction were not key ingredients to effective text-structure instruction (Hebert et al. 2016). The researchers concluded that these "nonsignificant effects should not be interpreted as indicating these instructional tools are not important. Rather, using signal words and explicit instruction techniques in TSI instruction is not expected to produce larger effects than interventions that use other instructional approaches used in these studies" (619).

So What? Actions for the Classroom

Start Text-Structure Instruction Early and Spiral

Akhondi, Malayeri, and Samad (2011) recommended that instruction should start with the descriptive text structure. However, we know from Williams and colleagues that second graders can absolutely learn comparison and cause and effect text structures (Williams et al. 2005; Williams et al. 2016). Oftentimes, in schools, we'll hear the recommendation to start with descriptive and sequential text structures in the primary grades because they are easier to learn. This recommendation has been echoed by Akholdi, Malayeri, and Samad (2011). However, there is no research that emphatically points to starting with one magic text structure. It is critical to note that even second graders can learn all five text structures. This leads us to recommend that teachers prioritize the content, rather than the text structure, when mapping out the order of structures to teach.

Go Beyond Identification and Connect to Writing

Simply identifying whether a text has a cause-and-effect or compare-and-contrast text structure is not enough. Identification should be just the first step in the process, not the end goal. Students should use the structure as a tool to identify key ideas in the text and even monitor their comprehension. For example, can they use the text-structure frame in the form of a graphic organizer to help them recall how key details are related?

Teaching students to ask guiding questions associated with the text structures helps students identify important information from texts (Roehling et al. 2017). Teachers may create anchor charts that contain, in addition to clue or signal words, guiding questions for each text structure. For example, on a comparison anchor chart, the following questions may be included (Roehling et al. 2017): "What is being compared? How are they the same? How are they different? What features are being compared?"

Another practical tip for applying text structures is to incorporate them into informational writing. Students frequently struggle to organize their thoughts when writing. We often find that students' efforts result in descriptive writing full of interesting, albeit random, facts that default into a descriptive-like text structure.

> *I learned a lot about frogs and I learned they can be the size of a dinner plate. I also learned that poisonous frogs can kill 10 people or 20,000 mice. The most interesting thing I learned was frogs are also called newts.*
>
> **(student sample from Robbins and Hilden 2016, 42)**

Simply having background knowledge about a topic is not enough. Rather, Graham and Harris (2013) point out that students also need genre knowledge, which includes knowledge about text structures. In the above example, the teacher might work with students to align the text structure with their goals. Thus, a student might use a compare-and-contrast text structure to write about how frogs and newts are different and similar, a sequential text structure to discuss their life cycles, and a cause-and-effect text structure to describe how the frog's poison affects their prey. Teacher can first model how to use paragraph frames for the whole group, and then have students practice using these frames on related topics and texts in small groups or in pairs.

Gradually Increase Text Complexity

When first introducing text structures, begin by modeling with short, single-structured texts (Jones, Clark, and Reutzel 2016, as cited by Pyle et al. 2017). These texts should be on topics that are familiar to students. It may be helpful to teach students how text features and graphics provide useful clues. For example, time lines often accompany sequential text structures, but arrows in diagrams serve different functions and can be associated with different text structures. Arrows in cycle diagrams (e.g., water cycle or life cycle) may be associated with a sequential text structure, and arrows in flow diagrams may be used to depict cause-and-effect relationships (e.g., texts related to droughts and erosion).

If you choose to teach signal words to help students identify text structures, embed this instructional strategy with other components of effective text-structure instruction. While teaching signal words does not appear to be harmful, we also cannot recommend it as a must-do in text-structure instruction. We found the following advice helpful.

> First, signal words can be misleading. There are times when a signal word may appear in a passage without reflecting the passage's overall structure. Second, students may end up paying more attention to the signal words than they do to the content of the passage. (Roehling et al. 2017, 73)

We recognize that text-structure instruction is likely multicomponent and commonly includes teaching aids such as signal words and graphic organizers. We hope future research will study which of these components are key ingredients for effective text-structure instruction.

We encourage teachers and reading specialists to think about spiraling their text-structure instruction. While individual text structures may be initially introduced in second and third grade, it is important that students gradually apply their text-structure knowledge to increasingly more complex texts, including longer texts that have elements of multiple text structures and are about less-familiar topics (Pyle et al. 2017).

Connect and Spiral Text-Structure Instruction with the Content Areas

When mapping text-structure instruction into a curriculum guide, we encourage reading specialists and coaches to begin by examining their curriculum guides for social studies and science topics and to discuss the timing of content-area units. It could be that the cause-and-effect text structure might be initially taught in second grade in relationship to a unit on magnets, then reinforced in third grade in a science unit on food chains, and finally applied along with other text structures such as descriptive and compare-and-contrast when discussing layers of the ocean in fifth grade. In this way, text structures are serving their intended purpose to provide a meaningful, authentic framework to recall, connect, and organize new knowledge learned from text.

Cautions and Caveats

Similar to other comprehension-related topics in this book, the effects of teaching expository text structures were consistently higher for research-related measures as compared to standardized comprehension measures (Pyle et al. 2017). Pyle and colleagues proposed that standardized measures may not be sensitive enough to measure readers' growth on creating text-based representations of expository texts.

How can I effectively teach expository text structures, and when should this instruction start?

Effective for ALL Readers in Grades 2–5	Duration of Instruction	Connect to Writing	Gradually Increase Complexity
• Text structure instruction is effective for all readers, including MLs and striving readers! • Instruction can start in second grade.	• The sweet spot for instruction is between 11 to 20 hours. • This breaks down into 30 minutes per day, 4 days a week, for 6 to 10 weeks.	• Move beyond simply identifying text structures. • Incorporate text structure instruction into writing about content areas.	• Introduce text structures with short passages on familiar topics. • Gradually increase text complexity in terms of length, topic, and number of text structures.

This work should spiral across grades and content areas!

(Hebert et al. 2016; Pyle et al. 2017; Wijekumar et al. 2018)

Other Useful Resources

Akhondi, M., F. A. Malayeri, and A. A. Samad. 2011. "How to Teach Expository Text Structure to Facilitate Reading Comprehension." *The Reading Teacher* 64 (5): 368–372.

Graham, S., and K. R. Harris. 2013. "Designing an Effective Writing Program." In *Best Practices in Writing Instruction* (2nd ed.), edited by S. Graham, C. A. MacArthur, and J. Fitzgerald, 3–25. New York: Guilford.

Graham, S., and M. Hebert. 2010. *Writing to Read: Evidence for How Writing Can Improve Reading: A Report from Carnegie Corporation of New York.* Carnegie Corporation of New York Report. Washington, DC: Alliance for Excellent Education. carnegie.org/media/filer_public/9d/e2/9de20604-a055-42da-bc00-77da949b29d7/ccny_report_2010_writing.pdf.

Robbins, H. H., and K. Hilden. 2016. "Teaching Text Structures to Support Content-Area Reading and Writing." *Reading in Virginia* 38: 41–50.

Roehling, J. V., M. Hebert, J. R. Nelson, and J. J. Bohaty. 2017. "Text Structure Strategies for Improving Expository Reading Comprehension." *The Reading Teacher* 71 (1): 71–82.

Question 17

Is explicit instruction of sentence comprehension necessary, and if so, what should it look like?

Discussion from the Classroom

Kalayla, an experienced sixth grade teacher, recently asked us if explicit syntax instruction is beneficial for reading comprehension. Her district has mandated a program that focuses on explicit grammar instruction that includes identifying parts of speech and correcting grammatical errors. The district language arts coach said that intermediate grade students' writing samples demonstrated a need for basic mechanics and cited low reading-comprehension scores as another reason for adopting the program.

Kalayla had recently read a blog post from a prominent literacy researcher that emphatically stated that diagramming sentences does not improve students' writing. However, in professional development offered by her state's department of education, she learned about Scarborough's Reading Rope (2001) and the role that syntax plays in language comprehension. Kalayla is wondering what is the best way to teach sentence-level comprehension.

Background and Assumptions

Syntactic, or grammatical, knowledge is the ability to apply knowledge of word order and sentence structure when reading text. You may be familiar with the book *Eats, Shoots & Leaves*, which illustrates the difference a comma can make. A quick internet search reveals dozens of humorous memes illustrating grammar gone wrong. For example, picture the meanings of the following two sentences.

I find inspiration in cooking my family and my dog.

I find inspiration in cooking, my family, and my dog.

Teachers, especially those working with English learners, intuitively understand that word order matters. Syntactic awareness involves the ability to manipulate words in a sentence and is often measured by having students "fix" sentences where the words are not in order (MacKay et al. 2021). Syntactic awareness predicts students' reading comprehension even after controlling for factors such as word reading, phonological awareness, and verbal working memory in upper elementary students (Deacon and Kieffer 2018).

Teachers are also at least intuitively aware that sentence length and complexity increases along with grade level, which has been widely supported through research (e.g., Zheng et al. 2023). Placeholders for syntactic complexity, such as average sentence length, have long been used as part of text-leveling measures. However, we also know from research that explicit instruction of grammar, including systematically teaching parts of speech and diagramming sentences, does not necessarily improve students' writing (Graham et al. 2012).

Research Studies That Inform the Question

Deacon, S. H., and M. Kieffer. 2018. "Understanding How Syntactic Awareness Contributes to Reading Comprehension: Evidence from Mediation and Longitudinal Models." *Journal of Educational Psychology* 110 (1): 72–86.

Zheng, H., X. Miao, Y. Dong, and D.-C. Yuan. 2023. "The Relationship Between Grammatical Knowledge and Reading Comprehension: A Meta-Analysis." *Frontiers in Psychology* 14: 1098568.

Research Findings

A Strong, Consistent Relationship Exists Between Syntactic Knowledge and Reading Comprehension

Deacon and Kieffer (2018), in their longitudinal study of third and fourth graders' reading comprehension, concluded that the role of syntactic awareness is as strong as the roles of vocabulary and morphological awareness. This means that syntactic awareness *uniquely* contributes to students' reading comprehension. This relationship is not only found in English but exists across such languages as Chinese (Zheng et al. 2023).

Interestingly, syntactic awareness and word recognition were not correlated in Deacon and Kieffer's study of third and fourth grade students (2018).

The Relationship Between Syntax Knowledge and Reading Comprehension Strengthens as Grade Level Increases

Zheng, Miao, Dong, and Yuan (2023) conducted a meta-analysis of eighty-eight studies (sixty-two articles) in English and Chinese. Primary-grade students' syntactic knowledge and their comprehension was significantly correlated. Furthermore, this relationship between syntactic knowledge and comprehension continued to increase with grade level through the post-secondary level. This is not surprising given that syntactic complexity in texts increases with grade levels. Leveling systems have historically included quantitative measures that consider the number of words in a sentence, a placeholder for syntactic complexity.

So What? Actions for the Classroom

Teach Cohesive Ties

Cohesive ties "are words or phrases used to connect ideas between different parts of text" (Sedita 2020b, para. 2). These ties are important for sentence comprehension because they help readers connect information found in different clauses. While strong readers integrate information in sentences automatically and unconsciously, struggling readers typically do poorer on pronoun-related comprehension questions and cloze tasks that involve anaphors (Cain and Oakhill 2007). (*Anaphors* are words or phrases that stand in for or refer to an earlier word.) Sedita (2020b) shares the following three types of cohesive devices that can occur between or within sentences:

- Pronouns that refer back to a previously mentioned noun
  Example: ***Jim*** went out to the playground. ***He*** played on the swings.

- Substitution of a synonym for a previously mentioned noun
  Example: There was a lot of ***food***, but she only ate the ***bread***.

- Transition words and inter-clausal connectors such as *so* or *because*.
  Example: *Jim played on the swings.* ***Later****, Jim played ball.*
  Example: *Mary was late,* ***so*** *she took the bus. Mary was late* ***because*** *she took the bus.*

Teachers can point out these cohesive ties as part of the read-aloud process. A teacher might write a sentence that has a cohesive tie on the board and then have students draw arrows connecting the cohesive tie back to the antecedent it refers to.

Consider the following excerpt from Gail Gibbons' book, *Alligators and Crocodiles*:

> The warmth of the inside of the nest helps determine whether the newborns will be males or females. When the temperature of the nest is above 88° Fahrenheit (31° Celsius), most of the hatchlings will be males. When the temperature is lower, most will be females. (2010, 24)

The second and third sentences are comparing the temperatures that determine whether the newborn alligators and crocodiles will be male or female. The teacher may have students draw circles around and connect "most" with "newborns," and "lower" with "88° Fahrenheit" to show the relationships between these words.

Teachers may also wish to provide examples of sentences where the pronouns are deleted and then have students provide the appropriate pronouns. To read more about teaching cohesive ties, we refer you to Joan Sedita's blog post "What Are Cohesive Devices and How Do They Affect Comprehension?" (2020b).

Teach Sentence Combining and Reduction

Sentence combining benefits students' writing (Graham and Perin 2007) and provides hands-on experience rearranging, combining, and simplifying sentences in ways that develop syntactic awareness. After reading aloud a text, choose two related sentences to share. Then discuss with students how the sentences are related, modeling how to find a way to connect them. Again, we recommend a blog post by Joan Sedita, "Syntactic Awareness: Teaching Sentence Structure (Part 1)" (2020a), for additional practical tips on teaching sentence combining and reduction. The following questions may provide inspiration for an anchor chart (Geiger, n.d.).

- → Do the sentences have similar or different ideas?
- → Does the second sentence provide more information?
- → Does one sentence provide an explanation?
- → Do the sentences show events in a sequence?

Consider another example from Gail Gibbons' *Alligators and Crocodiles*.

> **An American Alligator's Nest**
> The female lays about forty-five eggs on a bed of leaves and grasses.
>
> **An American Crocodile's Nest**
> The female digs a hole in the ground and lays about fifty eggs. (2010, 23)

After a read-aloud, the teacher may display these sentences on a projector and model how they share similar ideas. The teacher might model by saying, "These two sentences share something in common. They both share how many eggs are laid. They both start with 'The female.' I bet we could combine these two sentences into one." The students could then identify the key contrasting information and work in small groups to combine the sentences. One result might look like this: "The female alligator lays about forty-five eggs on leaves and grasses, whereas the crocodile lays fifty eggs in a hole." Notice the opportunity for the teacher to introduce a compare-contrast signal word, *whereas*, as a conjunction.

Teach Context Clues to Support Meaning, Not Decoding

The lack of relationship between word recognition and syntactic awareness in Deacon and Kieffer's (2018) study reinforces the finding that less capable readers (e.g., "poor readers") rely on sentence-level context clues to decode unfamiliar words (Stanovich 1980). While syntax awareness may help students infer meanings of unknown words, teachers should not encourage students to guess what a word says based primarily on context clues.

Identify Students for Remediation Who Have Difficulty Comprehending Complex Sentences

Scott and Balthazar (2013) recommend several practical, informal ways to identify students who regularly struggle to understand complex sentences. One way to check sentence-level comprehension is to ask individual students to paraphrase a complex sentence that they have just read. In the following example, a student has misunderstood the text and thinks that the attributes of Rachel Carson belong to different people (Scott and Balthazar 2013).

The text reads:
Rachel Carson, who was a scientist, writer, and ecologist, grew up in the rural river town of Springdale, Pennsylvania.

The teacher asks: "What do you know about Rachel Carson?"

The student paraphrases: "They grew up in the same place."

(Example from Scott and Balthazar 2013, 2)

Teachers can also look for evidence of sentence comprehension in students' writing samples. Scott and Balthazar recommend a practical rule of thumb that by age twelve, a student "should write sentences that are at least as long as spoken sentences, and sometimes longer" (2013, 7). When examining students' writing, they encourage teachers to ask whether sentences are of "sufficient length, complexity, and well-formedness (free of grammatical errors) for [their] age" (15).

Cautions and Caveats

Sentence comprehension is an area where the Science of Reading is farther along than the Science of Reading instruction (MacKay et al. 2021; Shanahan 2020). This means that while we know about the important role that syntax plays in comprehension, we know much less about the *who, when,* or *how* related to how to teach it. MacKay and colleagues noted that, while syntax instruction seems to be common in classrooms, there is currently "little accompanying evidence to determine whether these interventions are effective" (2021, 224). Therefore, be wary of claims that purport that syntax instructional resources found on lesson plan websites are based on the Science of Reading. Yes, we know that syntactic knowledge and awareness play an increasingly critical role in students' reading comprehension. However, we know much less about how to effectively support its development in the elementary grades.

We also note that the two focal studies in this section were not experimental studies of reading comprehension. They did not directly test the impact of syntax-related interventions. Deacon and Kieffer did a longitudinal study looking at how students' syntactic awareness predicts their reading comprehension. Zheng and colleagues used meta-analysis to calculate effect sizes to study correlations between grammatical knowledge and reading comprehension.

Should I teach comprehension at the sentence level?

Teach *cohesive* ties.

"When the temperature of the nest is above 88° Fahrenheit (31° Celsius), most of the hatchlings will be males. When the temperature is lower, most will be females."*

Teach sentence combining and reduction.

"An American Alligator's Nest: The female lays about forty-five eggs on a bed of leaves and grasses."*

"An American Crocodile's Nest: The female digs a hole in the ground and lays about fifty eggs."*

Teacher: *These two sentences share something in common. They both share how many eggs are laid. They both start with "The female." We can combine these two sentences into one!*

Research says:
- A positive and unique relationship exists between syntactic knowledge and reading comprehension, which strengthens across grade levels.

Where it fits:
- Start with mentor texts for read-alouds.
- Reinforce with students' writing examples.
- Follow up with small-group remediation instruction.

Alligators and Crocodiles by Gail Gibbons (2010)

Practical Tips for Sentence Comprehension

Model examples with these questions for sentence combining:

> The Third Little Pig was smart.
> The Third Little Pig built a house of bricks.

Books like *Eats, Shoots & Leaves* (Truss 2006) are great for modeling sentence reduction and combining.

- Do the sentences have **similar** or **different ideas**?
- Does the second sentence provide **more information**?
- Does one sentence provide an **explanation**?
- Do the sentences show events in a **sequence**? (example from *The Measured Mom*, Geiger 2024)

Avoid grammar worksheets that promote "skill and drill."

Ask students to paraphrase sentences they've just read.

The text reads:	The teacher asks:	The student paraphrases:
Rachel Carson, who was a scientist, writer, and ecologist, grew up in the rural river town of Springdale, Pennsylvania.	"What do you know about Rachel Carson?"	"They grew up in the same place."

(Scott and Balthazar 2013)

Other Useful Resources

Cain, K., and J. Oakhill, eds. 2007. *Children's Comprehension Problems in Oral and Written Language: A Cognitive Perspective.* New York: Guilford.

Geiger, A. n.d. "Syntax and Semantics in Structured Literacy." *The Measured Mom.* Accessed May 24, 2024. themeasuredmom.com/syntax-and-semantics-in-structured-literacy.

Gibbons, G. 2010. *Alligators and Crocodiles.* New York: Holiday House.

CONTINUED

Graham, S., D. McKeown, S. Kiuhara, and K. Harris. 2012. "A Meta-Analysis of Writing Instruction for Students in the Elementary Grades." *Journal of Educational Psychology* 104 (4): 879–896.

Graham, S., and D. Perin. 2007. *Writing Next: Effective Strategies to Improve Writing of Adolescents in Middle and High Schools.* Carnegie Corporation of New York Report. Washington, DC: Alliance for Excellent Education. media.carnegie.org/filer_public/3c/f5/3cf58727-34f4-4140-a014-723a00ac56f7/ccny_report_2007_writing.pdf

MacKay, E., E. Lynch, T. S. Duncan, and S. H. Deacon. 2021. "Informing the Science of Reading: Students' Awareness of Sentence-Level Information Is Important for Reading Comprehension." *Reading Research Quarterly* 56 (S1): S221–S230.

Scott, C. M., and C. Balthazar. 2013. "The Role of Complex Sentence Knowledge in Children with Reading and Writing Difficulties." *Perspectives on Language and Literacy* 39 (3): 18–30.

Sedita, J. 2020a. "Syntactic Awareness: Teaching Sentence Structure (Part 1). *The Keys to Literacy Blog*, June 2, 2020. keystoliteracy.com/blog/syntactic-awareness-teaching-sentence-structure-part-1/.

Sedita, J. 2020b. "What Are Cohesive Devices and How Do They Affect Comprehension?" *The Keys to Literacy Blog*, August 19, 2020. keystoliteracy.com/blog/what-are-cohesive-devices-and-how-do-they-affect-comprehension/.

Shanahan, T. 2020. "What Constitutes a Science of Reading Instruction?" *Reading Research Quarterly* 55 (1): S235–S247.

Stanovich, K. E. 1980. "Toward an Interactive-Compensatory Model of Individual Differences in the Development of Reading Fluency." *Reading Research Quarterly* 16 (1), 32–71.

Truss, L., and B. Timmons. 2006. *Eats, Shoots & Leaves: Why, Commas Really Do Make a Difference!* New York: G. P. Putnam's Sons Books for Young Readers.

Question 18

How do executive skills and cognitive flexibility impact students' reading comprehension, and how can I improve those skills?

Discussion from the Classroom

As teacher educators and frequent conference presenters, we have both met teachers who ask for advice about "conundrums" consisting of students who are failing to make progress despite the teacher trying all the latest evidence-based practices. Specifically with regard to this question, we have encountered teachers who describe upper elementary students who accurately decode words and read fluently but struggle with comprehension. These teachers will often say that these students struggle to retell the story in order from beginning to end, to answer inferential questions, and to identify the main ideas despite having been taught reading comprehension strategies. When we hear these "conundrums," we'll often ask questions about students' language skills (e.g., verbal reasoning, vocabulary) and about the students' executive functioning in school and specifically when reading.

When we ask teachers what they know about executive functioning, they often paint a picture of students who lack these skills. The students are described as having difficulty sustaining attention and becoming easily distracted when reading. They will often dive into an academic task with little attention to the goals or directions and may not have a plan for how to reach the end goal. One middle school teacher, in describing a student's lack of organization stated, "If their mind looks anything like their locker, it's a wonder they find anything!" We love Cartwright's description of "smart but scattered" students

(2023, 12). These "what's missing" anecdotes from teachers accurately point to the group of neurocognitive processes that we use in complex, goal-directed tasks called *executive functions*.

Background and Assumptions

Executive functions are mental or cognitive tools that people use to manage and monitor their thinking and achieve their goals (Cartwright 2023). Executive skills begin to emerge early in life and continue to develop across the school years. There are three core skills associated with executive functioning that work together (Cartwright 2023):

- **Cognitive flexibility** is the ability to actively shift attention between activities or different components of a task. Students might be asked, for example, to sort animals according to where they live and then switch to sorting according to whether they have feathers, scales, or fur.

- **Working memory** is our capacity to hold information in the mind and work with part of it. This is required, for example, when teachers ask students to read and then summarize a story in order, including beginning, middle, and end.

- **Inhibition** is the ability to think before acting. It means ignoring extraneous or distracting information and resisting a "habitual response" (Cartwright 2023). Inhibition is involved when students have to apply context to a multiple meaning word. For example, a reader must resist thinking about "beans" when they read about a "pod" of whales.

Additional, more-complex executive skills also contribute to reading, including planning, organization, and social understanding (Cartwright 2023).

Executive Functioning Training and Measurement

When researchers study executive functioning (EF), they use two types of tasks: general tasks that are not related to a specific domain or subject (e.g., sorting tasks that require manipulating visual shapes) and domain-specific tasks—in this case, reading-specific tasks (e.g., sorting words by decoding pattern versus by meaning).

Cognitive Flexibility

Research that investigates the role that executive functions play in reading development and intervention is still very much evolving. In this section, we will focus on one type of executive function, cognitive flexibility, where a growing body of intervention research exists. Card games such as rummy, Rummikub, cribbage, and Uno all require high levels of cognitive flexibility because they involve simultaneously keeping track of multiple combinations of cards according to both their suit and their number order. Good card players are often able to effortlessly switch or adapt their hands according to the evolving play.

Cognitive flexibility affects reading any time a reader shifts their focus between sources of information or features in the text. For example, readers must simultaneously connect the letters to their sounds to decode, while also paying attention to the meaning of words. This is called *graphophonological-semantic cognitive flexibility* (GSF). In some instances, readers may have difficulty shifting between meanings of polysemous, or multiple-meaning, words, such *fly*, *club*, and *volume*. Cognitive flexibility may also be involved when readers shift between strategies used when encountering a particularly difficult, dense text or when they shift attention between graphics and text in an effort to integrate information.

Research Studies That Inform the Question

Cartwright, K. B., A. M. Bock, J. H. Clause, E. A. C. August, H. G. Saunders, and K. J. Schmidt. 2020. "Near- and Far-Transfer Effects of an Executive Function Intervention for 2nd- to 5th-Grade Struggling Readers." *Cognitive Development* 56: 100932.

Cartwright, K. B., E. A. Coppage, A. B. Lane, T. Singleton, T. R. Marshall, C. Bentivegna. 2017. "Cognitive Flexibility Deficits in Children with Specific Reading Comprehension Difficulties." *Contemporary Educational Psychology* 50: 33–44.

Peng, P. 2023. "The Role of Executive Function in Reading Development and Reading Intervention." *Mind, Brain, and Education* 17 (4): 246–256.

Peng, P., and D. Fuchs. 2017. "A Randomized Control Trial of Working Memory Training with and without Strategy Instruction: Effects on Young Children's Working Memory and Comprehension." *Journal of Learning Disabilities* 50 (1): 62–80.

Zhang, Z., and P. Peng. 2023. "Longitudinal Reciprocal Relations Among Reading, Executive Function, and Social-Emotional Skills: Maybe Not for All." *Journal of Educational Psychology* 115 (3): 475–501. doi.org/10.1037/edu0000787.

Zheng, H., X. Miao, Y. Dong, and D.-C. Yuan. 2023. "The Relationship between Grammatical Knowledge and Reading Comprehension: A Meta-Analysis." *Frontiers in Psychology* 14: 1098568.

Research Findings

Language- or Reading-Specific Executive-Functioning Training Is Effective

Not surprisingly, when EF tasks are related to a specific skill, like reading, they are more likely to improve reading outcomes (Melby-Lervåg and Hulme 2013). Emerging research points to the importance of including reading-specific executive-functioning tasks as part of intervention work. In an intervention study of first graders, Peng and Fuchs (2017) found that ten sessions of one-to-one training on verbal working memory tasks resulted in students' improved listening comprehension (as measured by the Qualitative Reading Inventory).

Executive Functions and Reading Growth Go Hand in Hand for Advanced Readers

In a longitudinal study of students in grades 2 through 5, Zheng and Peng (2023) found a positive, synergistic relationship between executive functioning and reading for high-performing readers, and also found that this relationship strengthened with grade level. Peng suggests that "strong readers improve their reading not only through fast, efficient accumulation of reading skills and knowledge but also likely through mutualism between reading and EF" (2023, 249). However, this same positive relationship was missing for students with reading disabilities (Zhang and Peng 2023). Similarly, a longitudinal study found first graders with stronger executive skills had better expository comprehension by fourth grade (Wu et al. 2020). Interestingly, these authors also found executive skills predicted expository, but not narrative comprehension. Regularly reading complex texts requires students to engage their developing executive skills. In return, improved executive functioning allows students to persist and tackle more challenging reading tasks. For example, as students read longer, denser informational texts in the content areas, they are required to organize related information and ignore extraneous details while holding onto key information. As they practice, develop, and find success in engaging in these executive functioning skills, these same abilities allow students to tackle more complex texts, resulting in a positive spiral between academic reading and executive functioning.

Brief Cognitive Flexibility Interventions Can Improve Reading Comprehension

Cartwright designed a reading-related assessment and brief intervention for graphophonological-semantic cognitive flexibility (Cartwright 2010). The assessment requires students to sort a set of twelve word cards by meaning and initial sound into a 2 × 2 matrix.

Students' ability to switch back and forth between beginning sounds (words that start with /b/ and /t/) and meaning (animals versus forms of transportation) significantly contributes to students' reading comprehension across the elementary grades and languages (Cartwright 2023). This assessment has been used in brief, five-day interventions where students are trained using the same sorting matrix. When teachers in grades 2–5 administered this five-day cognitive flexibility intervention in small groups, striving readers significantly improved in reading comprehension in both school-based and standardized measures of comprehension (Cartwright et al. 2020). Further, when third graders with reading comprehension difficulties (they had adequate decoding skills but were at least a year behind in reading comprehension) received the intervention, their reading comprehension significantly improved (Cartwright et al. 2017). The sample sizes were small in these two studies. However, this research points to a promising line of EF intervention research, especially because the interventions were delivered by teachers.

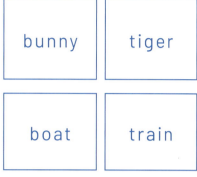

Figure 18.1. Example of Correct Sort on Cognitive Flexibility Task

Source: Cartwright et al. 2017, 38.

So What? Actions for the Classroom

New research related to this topic is being published almost monthly in reading, special education, and educational research journals, evolving our understanding of the relationship between executive functions and reading. That said, much less research has been conducted on executive-function instruction and interventions in reading. The Science of Reading instruction is still very much in development in this area. For a deeper dive on research-supported, practical tips for teaching executive functions, we recommend reading Kelly Cartwright's book *Executive Skills and Reading Comprehension: A Guide for Educators* (2023).

Assess and Remediate Cognitive Flexibility

The preliminary research around GSF flexibility is promising to the point where we will recommend that teachers assess striving readers' cognitive flexibility, especially when they have adequate decoding skills. If students demonstrate a weakness in cognitive flexibility, they may benefit from cognitive flexibility training specific to reading (Cartwright 2023; Cartwright et al. 2010). It is noteworthy that the same assessment materials and procedures described above can be used in this brief intervention. Each day of the five-day intervention, students work with a new set of words. They first sort words into two piles according to the two dimensions, initial sound and meaning. Then students complete the 2 × 2 matrix sort, where three of the cards are presented and they must choose a word that completes the matrix (see Cartwright 2010 for materials and directions).

Cartwright (2023) also provides additional practical tips for improving cognitive flexibility in the classroom. She recommends including wordplay riddles that require switching between meanings of polysemous words and exploring homonyms (such as the multiple meanings of the words *fork* and *jam*) and working with compound words (e.g., creating literal images for words like *butterfly*). Extending word sorts is another avenue for tapping into students' developing cognitive flexibility. For example, if students are sorting words according to long-vowel patterns, they may also sort according to part of speech (noun versus verb). Finally, Cartwright recommends including peer discussions of metaphors and idioms. Books like Tedd Arnold's *More Parts* and *Even More Parts*, which are full of humorous, literal illustrations of body-related idioms such as "I've got my eye on you," are entertaining for students while also encouraging students' developing cognitive flexibility.

Figure 18.2. Example of the Matrix Completion Task for Cognitive Flexibility Intervention

Source: Cartwright et al. 2017, 40.

Caveats and Cautions

→ Additional research is needed to study the impact of reading-specific executive functioning training, especially training delivered by teachers.

→ More research is needed to tease apart the relationships between executive functions and reading comprehension—for example, to unpack the relationships between executive functions and specific, targeted comprehension skills (such as inferring, summarizing, or even synthesizing information across multiple texts).

How can I improve students' cognitive flexibility and reading comprehension?

- **Cognitive flexibility** (CF) is a type of executive functioning that involves actively shifting attention between activities.
- **Graphophonological-semantic flexibility** (GSF), a subtype of CF, involves simultaneously connecting letters to sounds while also paying attention to meaning of words.

Brief GSF interventions delivered by teachers can improve reading comprehension.

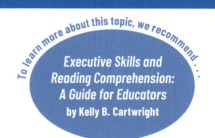

To learn more about this topic, we recommend...
Executive Skills and Reading Comprehension: A Guide for Educators by Kelly B. Cartwright

bus	
bird	tiger

Students sort words into two piles according to initial sounds and meaning. The word *truck* would complete the matrix.

Practical Tips to Boost Cognitive Flexibility
- Explore wordplay riddles and puns for polysemous words, homonyms, and compound words.
- Discuss idioms and metaphors in books such as *Even More Parts* (Arnold 2004).

Sources: Compiled from Wasik and Iannone-Campbell (2012); Hadley et al. (2022).

Other Useful Resources

Cartwright, K. B. 2023. *Executive Skills and Reading Comprehension: A Guide for Educators.* New York: Guilford.

Cartwright, K. B. 2010. *Word Callers: Small-Group and One-to-One Interventions for Children Who "Read" but Don't Comprehend.* Portsmouth, NH: Heinemann.

Melby-Lervåg, M., and C. Hulme. 2013. "Is Working Memory Training Effective? A Meta-Analytic Review." *Developmental Psychology* 49 (2): 270–291.

Wu, Y., L. A. Barquero, S. E. Pickren, A. T. Barber, and L. E. Cutting. 2020. "The Relationship Between Cognitive Skills and Reading Comprehension of Narrative and Expository Texts: A Longitudinal Study from Grade 1 to Grade 4." *Learning and Individual Differences* 80: 101848.

Question 19

How do I support my students' developing oral language?

Discussion from the Classroom

One of the benefits of the recent interest in Science of Reading is the renewed interest in students' developing oral language. Recently, Sarah, a kindergarten teacher, shared with us that many of her students, several of whom were multilingual learners, were not meeting the oral-language benchmark on the new state assessment. She shared her concern:

> "I've just always had quiet students. Some are just shy, while others have limited vocabularies because they are still learning English. Others didn't attend preschool and may not have had a lot of rich language at home. What can I do as a teacher to help build students' oral language as a classroom teacher? My reading block is ninety minutes and is already really full."

When we visited Sarah's classroom, we noticed that her literacy block involved a whole-group read-aloud of Steve Jenkins and Robin Page's informational book *What Do You Do with a Tail Like This?* She asked open-ended questions before, during, and after reading. However, we noticed that the same handful of students answered the majority of the questions while other students did not contribute to the discussion.

Background and Assumptions

→ Early language development is a critical contributor to students' decoding and later comprehension (Dickinson and Porche 2011; Kendeou et al. 2009). Language comprehension is featured prominently in reading theories such as the Simple View of Reading (Gough and Tunmer 1986) and the Active View of Reading (Duke and Cartwright 2021). Language comprehension is comprised of multiple factors, including background knowledge, vocabulary, language structures,

- verbal reasoning, and literacy knowledge, as famously depicted in Scarborough's Reading Rope (Scarborough 2001). (See Kambach and Mesmer (2024) for a practical guide on what these factors entail and how teachers can incorporate them into their comprehension instruction.)
- Much of the oral-language research in the past twenty years consists of descriptive and correlational studies that focus on the role that adults play in shaping children's language development. Recent research focusing on small-group interventions to improve preschoolers' and kindergartners' oral language is encouraging, but impacts are typically small (Phillips 2023).

Research Studies That Inform the Question

Hadley, E. B., E. M. Barnes, B. M. Wiernik, and M. Raghavan. 2022. "A Meta-Analysis of Teacher Language Practices in Early Childhood Classrooms." *Early Childhood Research Quarterly* 59: 186–202.

Hindeman, A. H., B. A. Wasik, and D. E. Bradley. 2019. "How Classroom Conversations Unfold: Exploring Teacher-Child Exchanges During Shared Book Reading." *Early Education and Development* 30 (4): 478–495.

Silverman, R. D., E. Johnson, K. Keane, and S. Khanna. 2020. "Beyond Decoding: A Meta-Analysis of the Effects of Language Comprehension Interventions on K–5 Students' Language and Literacy Outcomes." *Reading Research Quarterly* 55 (S1): S207–S233.

Research Findings

A recent meta-analysis reviewed forty-three language comprehension interventions for K–5 students (Silverman et al. 2020). The interventions included explicit instruction of vocabulary, morphology, and syntax on a variety of literacy outcomes. Together, these interventions had large positive effects on custom measures of vocabulary and smaller, modest effects on listening comprehension and reading comprehension. Most interesting, the authors found that multicomponent interventions (e.g., those that included vocabulary, morphology, and syntax) were more effective than those that only contained a single component, such as vocabulary. Also, intervention results did not differ by grouping size. Whole-group interventions were just as effective as small-group or even one-to-one interventions.

Hindeman, Wasik, and Bradley (2019) recorded read-alouds in Head Start classrooms to study the relationship between teachers' talk and students' vocabulary. They found that teacher talk in preschool read-alouds consisted mainly of close-ended questions that were consistently followed by no wait time and one-word student answers. Read-alouds with higher proportions of student talk predicted students' vocabulary growth. Surprisingly, the type of read-aloud question—open versus closed—was not associated with vocabulary growth. (Notice that this is an observational study and not an instructional intervention study.)

Hadley and colleagues (2022) conducted a meta-analysis that involved coding the types of teacher talk in preschool and kindergarten classrooms. They found that teacher talk falls into two main categories:

→ The **Emergent Academic Language** register includes teacher talk about concepts and abstract ideas that go beyond the here and now. This type of talk is also characterized by longer, more complex sentences and a greater variety of words, and it includes teacher modeling of academic talk. ("Let's predict, or guess, what type of animal might have flat, blue feet like this picture.")

→ **Bridging Language** includes teacher talk that encourages students to extend and scaffolds students' talk.

These two types of talk were distinctly independent from one another. Interestingly, both types of talk were related to vocabulary talk (providing definitions and examples of words, calling attention to words, and so on).

So What? Actions for the Classroom

Increase Interactive Talk and Student Turn-Taking

Students' language grows through use. This means that as teachers we want to make sure that we are acting as facilitators of conversations. We do this when we include lots of open-ended questions followed up by back-and-forth conversational turn-taking. Hindeman, Wasik, and Bradley note that "the value of a question depends at least partly on children's opportunities to answer it" (2019, 481). Too often, a great open-ended question is wasted when only one child responds and the teacher moves immediately onto the next question. Instead, open-ended questions need to be viewed as invitations to explore a concept using students' developing language through multiple turn-taking. Such interactive talk is responsive and encourages students to stretch their developing vocabulary and syntax in ways that promote academic language.

When teachers ask open-ended questions and then use a range of responsive prompts, they increase the likelihood that students will continue to participate in conversations.

Figure 19.1. Examples of Teacher Talk That Promotes Students' Oral Language

Type of Teacher Response	Purpose	Sample Teacher Talk During a Read-Aloud of *What Do You Do with a Tail Like This?* (Jenkins and Page 2008)
Expansions and extensions: teacher extends the students' original language	Modeling academic language	Student: [Points to picture of foot] "Monkey." Teacher: "You think that foot belongs to a monkey. Let's look and see if you're right!"
Elicitations	Questions or requests that encourage students to engage in additional conversation or turn-taking	S: "Skunk tail—stinky!" [Points to skunk tail] T: "Why do you think skunks lift their tails?"
Extended wait time	After asking a question, the teacher waits 3–5 seconds before calling on a student.	
High-level questions	Questions that ask for abstract thinking, including inferential, open-ended questions, and questions about vocabulary. These questions go beyond one word, right or wrong answers.	"How are your ears different than the animal ears on this page?"
Responsive talk	Talk in response to a student's comment, which can include repeating, confirming the comment, and active listening	"That's right, Thomas, the rabbit's ears are long, and Trey said they are fuzzy. What great words to describe the rabbit's ears."

Sources: Compiled from Wasik and Iannone-Campbell (2012); Hadley et al. (2022).

Assess Your Talk Moves

Assessing our teacher talk can provide needed insight into how frequently we are engaging in interactive talk with our students and whether we are regularly having interactive conversations with *all* of our students. Hadley, Newman, and Mock (2020) recommend that teachers record how many times they have had extended conversations, defined as at least five turns, with each student in the classroom over the course of the week. This self-assessment makes "talk deserts" with individual students more visible and trackable over time. Small-group time is perfect for fitting in these interactive conversations. Teachers can also assess how many conversational turns they are typically engaging in during shared book readings and whole-group content-area lessons. To help set teacher talk goals, a reading specialist could observe a preschool teacher's informational read-aloud and record the number of conversational turns and the types of responses the teacher uses.

Try the TALK Acronym

Hadley, Newman, and Mock (2020) have compiled many of these practical recommendations into the TALK acronym:

How do I support my students' developing oral language?

Try the **TALK** strategy during small groups and read-alouds.

Take turns and "strive for five."
- Extend wait time and extend conversations (five or more turns).
- Replace "Good thinking" with "I wonder why."

Ask open-ended questions.
- Ask "how" and "why" questions.
- "What do you think will happen next?"

Listen to students' responses.
- Build on students' comments and interests (echo and add).
  Student: "It's tall!"
  Teacher: "Look at how tall your building is! How many blocks did you use?"

Keep track of rich responses.
- Tally student responses and types of teacher-talk.

(Hadley, Newman, and Mock 2020)

Other Useful Resources

Dickinson, D. K., and M. V. Porche. 2011. "Relation Between Language Experiences in Preschool Classrooms and Children's Kindergarten and Fourth-Grade Language and Reading Abilities." *Child Development* 82 (3): 870–886.

Duke, N. K., and K. B. Cartwright. 2021. "The Science of Reading Progresses: Communicating Advances Beyond the Simple View of Reading." *Reading Research Quarterly* 56 (S1): S25–S44.

Gough, P. B., and W. E. Tunmer. 1986. "Decoding, Reading, and Reading Disability." *Remedial and Special Education* 7 (1): 6–10.

Hadley, E. B., K. M. Newman, and J. Mock. 2020. "Setting the Stage for TALK: Strategies for Encouraging Language-Building Conversations." *The Reading Teacher* 74 (1): 39–48.

Herrera, S., B. M. Phillips, Y. Newton, J. L. Dombek, and J. A. Hernandez. 2021. *Effectiveness of Early Literacy Instruction: Summary of 20 Years of Research (REL 2021-084)*. U.S. Department of Education, Institute of Education Sciences, National Center for Education Evaluation and Regional Assistance, Regional Educational Laboratory Southeast.

Jenkins, J. R., J. A. Peyton, E. A. Sanders, and P. Vadasy. 2004. "Effects of Reading Decodable Texts in Supplemental First Grade Tutoring." *Scientific Studies of Reading* 8 (1): 53–85.

Jenkins, S., and R. Page. 2008. *What Do You Do with a Tail Like This?* New York: Scholastic.

Kambach, A. E., and H. A. Mesmer. 2024. "Comprehension for Emergent Readers: Revisiting the Reading Rope." *The Reading Teacher* 77 (6): 888–898.

Kendeou, P., P. van den Broek, M. J. White, and J. S. Lynch. 2009. "Predicting Reading Comprehension in Early Elementary School: The Independent Contributions of Oral Language and Decoding Skills." *Journal of Educational Psychology* 101 (4): 765–778.

Phillips, B. M. 2023. "Language Interventions in Early Childhood: Summary and Implications from a Multistudy Program of Research." In *Handbook on the Science of Early Literacy*, edited by S. Neuman, S. Q. Cabell, and N. P. Terry, 139–150. New York: Guilford.

Scarborough, H. S. 2001. "Connecting Early Language and Literacy to Later Reading (Dis)abilities: Evidence, Theory, and Practice." In *Handbook of Early Literacy Research* (Vol. 1), edited by S. B. Neuman and D. K. Dickinson, 97–110. New York: Guilford.

Wasik, B. A., and C. Iannone-Campbell. 2012. "Developing Vocabulary Through Purposeful, Strategic Conversations." *The Reading Teacher* 66 (4): 321–332.

Question 20

Should I match students to books by reading level? If so, how?

Discussion from the Classroom

"Every reader must be taught in grade-level materials," the state website mandated in all-bold print on the grant application. Carla, a third grade teacher in an urban school with a high number of multilingual learners, agonized, "Do they want these kids to *read* these books? Because most of my third grade readers are on a first grade level, and I don't think putting a third grade book in front of them will magically turn them into third grade readers. Sure, I can scaffold, but at what point is my scaffolding just *me* doing all the reading? I can expose them, but is that going to help them become readers?"

We feel Carla's pain, and we've been there. We agree that students, especially multilingual learners, should not be limited in their language and knowledge development by their decoding skills. Students need to develop vocabulary, knowledge about the world, and in-depth comprehension as they are learning to decode. But "everyone-in-third-grade-gets-the-third-grade-book" is a problem. There certainly is research showing that kids get tracked into groups and limited by their reading levels (Puzio, Colby, and Algeo-Nichols 2020), but there is also evidence that kids need to read a large volume of text that they *can* read in order to advance (Allington and McGill-Franzen 2021).

In some respects, the research suggests that the question "Should I match students to books by reading level?" misses several important variables that we unpack below. Having the answer to this question alone does not guide practice. Teachers must also think about who the readers are developmentally, what kinds of instructional supports might be offered, and what elements of reading are being considered (e.g., decoding, fluency, comprehension).

Background and Assumptions

Reader-text matching has been a focus for classroom teachers for some time, and yet many common practices related to such matching do not have strong research support. For readers beyond the beginning stages, teachers have operationalized student reading levels based on the percentages of words in a text they read accurately: independent text (95 percent and up), instructional text (90 to 94 percent), and frustrational text (below 90 percent). These levels emerged from clinical work done by Betts (1946), but until very recently, their basis was not empirical—not based on research (Burns 2024). In studies, these parameters have been tested out, and, depending on instructional conditions and student variables, can be flexed.

Another approach to reader-text matching has been readability formulas. Readability formulas predict a text's difficulty by analyzing features of its words and sentences (e.g., frequency of words, length of sentences). The appropriate text level for a student is commonly associated with comprehension of 70 to 75 percent (Mesmer 2008). The labels used to express this difficulty are grades and months (e.g., 2.3, 2.4, 2.5), which sound rather precise, but the formulas have a standard error of measure between .5 and 1.0 grades.

Text difficulty has different meaning in beginning reading when students have not gained mastery of the most common graphemes in English. With readers at the beginning stages, texts may be adjusted to contain a proportion of words matching graphemes that the reader knows, as well as known high-frequency words. These are described as highly decodable texts (see Question 7).

Research Studies That Inform the Question

Amendum, S. J., K. Conradi, and E. Hiebert. 2018. "Does Text Complexity Matter in the Elementary Grades? A Research Synthesis of Text Difficulty and Elementary Students' Reading Fluency and Comprehension." *Educational Psychology Review* 30 (1): 121–151.

O'Connor, R. E., K. M. Bell, K. R. Harty, L. K. Larkin, S. M. Sackor, and N. Zigmond. 2002. "Teaching Reading to Poor Readers in the Intermediate Grades: A Comparison of Text Difficulty." *Journal of Educational Psychology* 94 (3): 474–485.

O'Connor, R. E., H. L. Swanson, and C. Geraghty. 2010. "Improvement in Reading Rate Under Independent and Difficult Text Levels: Influences on Word and Comprehension Skills." *Journal of Educational Psychology* 102 (1): 1–19.

Vadasy, P. F., and E. A. Sanders. 2009. "Supplemental Fluency Intervention and Determinants of Reading Outcomes." *Scientific Studies of Reading* 13 (5): 383–425.

Vadasy, P. F., E. A. Sanders, and J. A. Peyton. 2005. "Relative Effectiveness of Reading Practice or Word-Level Instruction in Supplemental Tutoring: How Text Matters." *Journal of Learning Disabilities* 38 (4): 364–380.

Research Findings

Generally, Readers Are Less Accurate and Less Fluent as Text Difficulty Increases

In a review of the literature (not a meta-analysis), researchers examined twenty-six articles in which "text level," "text complexity," "reading level," "text difficulty," and similar terms appeared (Amendum, Conradi, and Hiebert 2018). They found mostly quasi-experimental studies in which researchers measured text difficulty and examined effects on decoding, comprehension, and fluency. The studies in this collection characterized text difficulty in numerous ways, with some using word-accuracy levels (e.g., less than 90 percent, 90 to 95 percent, 95 percent and up), others using readability, some using decodability, and still others using generically described high and low levels. About 90 percent of the studies found a negative relationship between text difficulty and accuracy. As texts got more difficult, accuracy went down, regardless of how the study authors characterized text difficulty. Over 70 percent of the studies found the same with respect to fluency; as texts got more difficult, fluency went down.

In an experimental study with struggling second and third grade readers, researchers examined the impact of an intervention on fluency, decoding, and comprehension (Vadasy and Sanders 2009). They analyzed the decodability of each word in each text using an orthographic complexity scale (e.g., simple: *cat, strip*; harder: *charge, team*; hardest: *pretreatment*). These results also showed that readers' decoding, fluency, and comprehension were better in texts with less-complex words. For struggling second and third graders in small-group tutoring, decoding, fluency, and comprehension were better in easier texts.

In contrast to these findings, researchers conducted an experiment that explicitly tested fluency, word recognition, and comprehension using different text difficulty levels for struggling second through fourth graders (O'Connor, Swanson, and Geraghty 2010). Three times per week, for fifteen minutes, the groups read to an adult listener. One group read aloud materials at their independent reading level (92–100 percent accuracy) and the other group read aloud materials at a difficult reading level (80–90 percent accuracy). Adult listeners provided words that the students could not read but did not teach decoding. Both groups did significantly better than a no-treatment control group. At the end of twenty weeks, there were no differences in fluency between the 92–100 percent group and the 80–90 percent group. It's important to remember that whenever these students did not know how to decode a word, an adult listener would provide it. So, regardless of the condition, difficult words were provided.

Increasing Text Difficulty Does Not Appear to Improve Comprehension, but Findings Are Mixed

With respect to comprehension, in about half of the studies, increases in text difficulty were associated with declines in comprehension (Amendum, Conradi, and Heibert 2018). In no studies did increases in text difficulty *improve* comprehension, and in a little under half there was no relationship between difficulty and comprehension (Amendum, Conradi, and Heibert 2018). In an experiment of struggling second to fourth graders, decreases in difficulty were associated with better comprehension as measured by a cloze task (Vadasy and Sanders 2009). One disadvantage of cloze tests is that, because they require students to "fill in the blanks" with missing words, they test only sentence-level comprehension. In general, teachers should not increase text difficulty to improve comprehension, especially for struggling readers; in some cases, there is no support for it, and in others it is detrimental.

Beginning and Struggling Students Are More Sensitive to Text Difficulty, but This Interacts with Levels of Support

In a study of struggling third through fifth grade students, researchers randomly assigned students to one of two groups: (a) classroom-leveled matched texts (e.g., reading texts at a 4.0 level if in grade 4) or (b) reading-leveled matched texts (e.g., reading texts at a 1.7 level based on assessments). After eighteen weeks of tutoring, the group of students in the reading-level matched texts were more fluent than the students in the classroom-level matched group. For struggling readers about two grade levels below their peers, the "every-third-grader-gets-the-third-grade-book" practice did not improve fluency (O'Connor et al. 2002).

In another study with struggling students, readers were less accurate and fluent with more complex words (Vadasy, Sanders, and Peyton 2005). However, with struggling readers who have an adult to decode unknown words, text difficulty was reduced (O'Connor, Swanson, and Geraghty 2010).

So What? Actions for the Classroom

Match Readers to Texts, but Observe and Flex

Should teachers match readers to texts? Yes! The research suggests that there are thresholds of difficulty. When the decoding demands are too high, comprehension and fluency will be lost. What is too high? The research suggests that with support (see below), readers may be able to handle texts that they initially decode with 80 percent accuracy. If students are being asked to read a text independently or at home, they should be able to read it with an accuracy level of closer to 90 percent.

What about grade levels for more advanced readers? Can these be used? Of course, but the key is how. The grade levels delivered by Lexile, Flesch-Kincaid, and other formulas are really ballpark figures. They have standard errors of measurement between one-half and one grade level. With no other information about a book, these grade levels provide a place to start, but observation and instructional flexing is essential. That means observing students' accuracy, fluency, and comprehension and then stepping in with instructional supports if a text is too hard.

Imagine you are teaching a group of third graders; about 10 percent are reading significantly above grade level, 50 percent are at grade level, 30 percent below, and 10 percent significantly below grade level. You have them read a book labeled 3.5. The true difficulty of the book could be as high as 4.5 or as low as 2.5. Once they begin reading, the 10 percent significantly below level will likely need decoding help, and, depending on the book's true difficulty, many of the students at grade level may as well. You observe. With that 10 percent, you listen to them read and then provide access or decoding support. You informally assess comprehension, each day, asking yourself, "Are the students missing basic facts?" Then you flex. If they struggle with word recognition, then you could support decoding. Or if the book is significantly too hard, you could read it aloud and provide another text for their reading.

The point is this: the levels are only a starting place. Active observation and instructional responses are essential.

Pay More Attention to Texts and Supports When Matching Beginners or Struggling Readers

The research suggests that what makes a text difficult differs based on developmental levels. Essentially, students at the beginning levels are going to struggle with word-level accuracy and fluency due to their lack of reading experience and decoding knowledge. This is why studies have analyzed the complexity of words—gaps in letter-sound knowledge and morphological patterns compromise accuracy and fluency.

Readers may not have seen as many words and/or they may not know all the patterns. Beginning readers who are reading at primer to grade 2 levels are still learning the major graphemes for English, especially the vowel graphemes. Keep in mind that "beginning readers" might be typically developing students in kindergarten through grade 2 or beginners in higher grades reading at lower grade levels (e.g., a third grader reading at a first-grade level).

The research suggests three different practices to address potential accuracy and fluency issues. The first is to provide decoding support for unknown words. With students reading at 80 percent accuracy, this helped fluency development (O'Connor et al. 2002). Another support for decoding is rereading a text several times (Stahl and Heubach 2005).

The second practice is to pay attention to the complexity of the words that are in texts and the patterns in them. Watch out for books with words with multiple syllables or multi-letter vowel graphemes, because those words will impact accuracy and fluency.

The last practice is to adjust reading levels for students who are two levels *below* their assigned grade. In this scenario, research suggests that students would benefit from reading-level matched materials rather than classroom-level materials. For example, it is *not* recommended to expect a student in fourth grade who reads at a second-grade reading level to read accurately and fluently using fourth-grade materials. Keep in mind, however, that it is very important to make sure that this student can still access the ideas, vocabulary, and content in classroom materials through partner reading, listening, or some other mechanism. However, such materials would not constitute the reading diet.

Monitor Accuracy and Fluency as Text Difficulty Increases

Regardless of the metrics used to match readers to text (levels, readability [e.g., 2.2., 2.3., 2.4], or beginning text features), monitor accuracy and fluency levels whenever you are increasing text difficulty. For example, let's say your second grade students are reading a series of informational texts on life cycles. The first text is at a 2.4 readability level, but the next one is at a 3.0. Perusing the second one, you see words like *fertilize*, *amphibian*, and *ecosystem*. When you ask students to read this second book, listen to them read a paragraph or two. If they are unable to decode words or are slower than usual, use the scaffolds described above.

Other Useful Resources

Allington, R. L., and A. M. McGill-Franzen. 2021. "Reading Volume and Reading Achievement: A Review of Recent Research." *Reading Research Quarterly* 56 (1S): S231–S238.

Betts, E. 1946. *Foundations of Reading Instruction*. New York: American Book Co.

Burns, M. K. 2024. "Assessing an Instructional Level During Reading Fluency Interventions: A Meta-Analysis of the Effects on Reading." *Assessment for Effective Intervention*: 15345084241247064.

Puzio, K., G. T. Colby, and D. Algeo-Nichols. 2020. "Differentiated Literacy Instruction: Boondoggle or Best Practice?" *Review of Educational Research* 90 (4): 459–498.

Stahl, S. A., and K. Heubach. 2005. "Fluency-Oriented Reading Instruction." *Journal of Literacy Research* 37 (1): 25–60.

Treptow, M. A., M. K. Burns, and J. J. McComas. 2007. "Reading at the Frustration, Instructional, and Independent Levels: The Effects on Students' Reading Comprehension and Time on Task." *School Psychology Review* 36 (1): 159–166.

References

Akhondi, M., F. A. Malayeri, and A. A. Samad. 2011. "How to Teach Expository Text Structure to Facilitate Reading Comprehension." *The Reading Teacher* 64 (5): 368–372. doi.org/10.1598/RT.64.5.9.

Allington, R. L., and A. M. McGill-Franzen. 2021. "Reading Volume and Reading Achievement: A Review of Recent Research." *Reading Research Quarterly* 56 (1S): S231–S238. doi.org/10.1002/rrq.404.

Almasi, J. F., and S. J. Hart. 2019. "Best Practices in Narrative Text Comprehension Instruction." In *Best Practices in Literacy Instruction* (6th ed.), edited by L. M. Morrow and L. Gambrell, 221–249. New York: Guilford Press.

Amendum, S. J., K. Conradi, and E. Hiebert. 2018. "Does Text Complexity Matter in the Elementary Grades? A Research Synthesis of Text Difficulty and Elementary Students' Reading Fluency and Comprehension." *Educational Psychology Review* 30 (1): 121–151. doi.org/10.1007/s10648-017-9398-2.

Anderson, R. C., and W. E. Nagy. 1992. "The Vocabulary Conundrum." *American Educator* 16 (4): 14–18, 44–47.

Anthony, J. L., C. J. Lonigan, K. Driscoll, B. M. Phillips, and S. R. Burgess. 2003. "Phonological Sensitivity: A Quasi-Parallel Progression of Word Structure Units and Cognitive Operations." *Reading Research Quarterly* 38 (4): 470–487. doi.org/10.1598/RRQ.38.4.3.

Bhattacharya, A. 2020. "Syllabic versus Morphemic Analyses: Teaching Multisyllabic Word Reading to Older Struggling Readers." *Journal of Adolescent & Adult Literacy* 63 (5): 491–497. doi.org/10.1002/jaal.984.

Benjamin, R. G., and P. J. Schwanenflugel. 2010. "Text Complexity and Oral Reading Prosody in Young Readers." *Reading Research Quarterly* 45 (4): 388–404. doi.org/10.1598/RRQ.45.4.2.

Berninger, V. W., and D. Amtmann. 2003. "Preventing Written Expression Disabilities Through Early and Continuing Assessment and Intervention for Handwriting and/or Spelling Problems: Research into Practice." In *Handbook of Learning Disabilities* (1st ed.), edited by H. L. Swanson, K. R. Harris, and S. Graham, 345–363. New York: Guilford.

Betts, E. 1946. *Foundations of Reading Instruction*. New York: American Book Co.

Blachman, B. A., C. Schatschneider, J. M. Fletcher, D. J. Francis, S. M. Clonan, B. A. Shaywitz, and S. E. Shaywitz. 2004. "Effects of Intensive Reading Remediation for Second and Third Graders and a 1-year Follow-Up." *Journal of Educational Psychology* 96 (3): 444–461. doi.org/10.1037/0022-0663.96.3.444.

Boyer, N., and L. C. Ehri. 2011. "Contribution of Phonemic Segmentation Instruction with Letters and Articulation Pictures to Word Reading and Spelling in Beginners." *Scientific Studies of Reading* 15 (5): 440–470.

Brown, R., M. Pressley, P. Van Meter, and T. Schuder. 1996. "A Quasi-Experimental Validation of Transactional Strategies Instruction with Low-Achieving Second-Grade Readers." *Journal of Educational Psychology* 88 (1): 18–37. doi.org/10.1037/0022-0663.88.1.18.

Burns, M. K. 2024. "Assessing an Instructional Level During Reading Fluency Interventions: A Meta-Analysis of the Effects on Reading." *Assessment for Effective Intervention:* 15345084241247064.

Burns, M. K., N. K. Duke, and K. B. Cartwright. 2023. "Evaluating Components of the Active View of Reading as Intervention Targets: Implications for Social Justice." *School Psychology* 38 (1): 30–41. doi.org/10.1037/spq0000519.

Cain, K., and J. Oakhill, eds. 2007. *Children's Comprehension Problems in Oral and Written Language: A Cognitive Perspective*. New York: Guilford.

Cantrell, S. C., J. F. Almasi, M. Rintamaa, and J. C. Carter. 2016. "Supplemental Reading Strategy Instruction for Adolescents: A Randomized Trial and Follow-Up Study." *The Journal of Educational Research* 109 (1): 7–26. doi.org/10.1080/00220671.2014.917258.

Cartwright, K. B. 2010. *Word Callers: Small-Group and One-to-One Interventions for Children Who "Read" but Don't Comprehend*. Portsmouth, NH: Heinemann.

Cartwright, K. B. 2023. *Executive Skills and Reading Comprehension: A Guide for Educators*. New York: Guilford.

Cartwright, K. B., A. M. Bock, J. H. Clause, E. A. C. August, H. G. Saunders, and K. J. Schmidt. 2020. "Near- and Far-Transfer Effects of an Executive Function Intervention for 2nd- to 5th-Grade Struggling Readers." *Cognitive Development* 56: 100932. doi.org/10.1016/j.cogdev.2020.100932.

Cartwright, K. B., E. A. Coppage, A. B. Lane, T. Singleton, T. R. Marshall, C. Bentivegna. 2017. "Cognitive Flexibility Deficits in Children with Specific Reading Comprehension Difficulties." *Contemporary Educational Psychology* 50: 33–44. doi.org/10.1016/j.cedpsych.2016.01.003.

Cartwright, K. B., T. R. Marshall, K. L. Dandy, and M. C. Isaac. 2010. "The Development of Graphophonological-Semantic Cognitive Flexibility and Its Contribution to Reading Comprehension in Beginning Readers." *Journal of Cognition and Development* 11 (1): 61–85. doi.org/10.1080/15248370903453584.

Castiglioni-Spalten, M. L., and L. C. Ehri. 2003. "Phonemic Awareness Instruction: Contribution of Articulatory Segmentation to Novice Beginners' Reading and Spelling." *Scientific Studies of Reading* 7 (1): 25–52.

Cervetti, G. N., M. S. Fitzgerald, E. Hiebert, and M. Hebert. 2023. "Meta-Analysis Examining the Impact of Vocabulary Instruction on Vocabulary Knowledge and Skill." *Reading Psychology* 44 (6): 672–709. doi.org/10.1080/02702711.2023.2179146.

Cheatham, J. P., and J. H. Allor. 2012. "The Influence of Decodability in Early Reading Text on Reading Achievement: A Review of the Evidence." *Reading and Writing* 25 (9): 2223–2246. doi.org/10.1007/s11145-011-9355-2.

Clay, M. M. 1989. "Concepts about Print in English and Other Languages." *The Reading Teacher* 42 (4): 268–276.

Clay, M. M. 1991. *Becoming Literate: The Construction of Inner Control*. Portsmouth, NH: Heinemann.

Colenbrander, D., H. C. Wang, T. Arrow, and A. Castles. 2020. "Teaching Irregular Words: What We Know, What We Don't Know, and Where We Can Go from Here." *The Educational and Developmental Psychologist* 37 (2): 97–104.

Deacon, S. H., and M. Kieffer. 2018. "Understanding How Syntactic Awareness Contributes to Reading Comprehension: Evidence from Mediation and Longitudinal Models." *Journal of Educational Psychology* 110 (1): 72–86. doi.org/10.1037/edu0000198.

Dehaene, S. 2009. *Reading in the Brain: The New Science of How We Read*. New York: Penguin Random House.

Dewitz, P., J. Jones, and S. Leahy. 2009. "Comprehension Strategy Instruction in Core Reading Programs." *Reading Research Quarterly* 44 (2): 102–126. doi.org/10.1598/RRQ.44.2.1.

Dickinson, D. K., and M. V. Porche. 2011. "Relation Between Language Experiences in Preschool Classrooms and Children's Kindergarten and Fourth-Grade Language and Reading Abilities." *Child Development* 82 (3): 870–886.

Dinehart, L. H. 2015. "Handwriting in Early Childhood Education: Current Research and Future Implications." *Journal of Early Childhood Literacy* 15 (1): 97–118. doi.org/10.1177/1468798414522825.

Dolch, E. W. 1936. "A Basic Sight Vocabulary." *The Elementary School Journal* 36 (6): 456–460. doi.org/10.1086/457353.

Drouin, M., S. L. Horner, and T. A. Sondergeld. 2012. "Alphabet Knowledge in Preschool: A Rasch Model Analysis." *Early Childhood Research Quarterly* 27 (3): 543–554. doi.org/10.1016/j.ecresq.2011.12.008.

Duke, N. K., and K. B. Cartwright. 2021. "The Science of Reading Progresses: Communicating Advances Beyond the Simple View of Reading." *Reading Research Quarterly* 56 (S1): S25–S44. doi.org/10.1002/rrq.411.

Duke, N. K., and N. M. Martin. 2011. "10 Things Every Literacy Educator Should Know About Research." *The Reading Teacher* 65 (1): 9–22.

Ehri, L. C. 2005. "Learning to Read Words: Theory, Findings, and Issues." *Scientific Studies of Reading* 9 (2): 167–188.

Ehri, L. C. 2014. "Orthographic Mapping in the Acquisition of Sight Word Reading, Spelling Memory, and Vocabulary Learning." *Scientific Studies of Reading* 18 (1): 5–21. doi.org/10.1080/10888438.2013.819356.

Ehri, L. C., S. R. Nunes, D. M. Willows, B. V. Schuster, Z. Yaghoub-Zadeh, and T. Shanahan. 2001. "Phonemic Awareness Instruction Helps Children Learn to Read: Evidence from the National Reading Panel's Meta-Analysis." *Reading Research Quarterly* 36 (3): 250-287.

Ehri, L. C., and J. Sweet. 1991. "Fingerpoint Reading of Memorized Text: What Enables Beginners to Process the Print?" *Reading Research Quarterly* 26 (4): 442–462.

Ehri, L. C., and L. S. Wilce. 1987. "Does Learning to Spell Help Beginners Learn to Read Words?" *Reading Research Quarterly* 22 (1): 47–65. doi.org/10.2307/747720.

Elbro, C., P. F. de Jong, D. Houter, and A. Nielsen. 2012. "From Spelling Pronunciation to Lexical Access: A Second Step in Word Decoding?" *Scientific Studies of Reading* 16 (4): 341–359. doi.org/10.1080/10888438.2011.568556.

Ellefson, M. R., R. Treiman, and B. Kessler. 2009. "Learning to Label Letters by Sounds or Names: A Comparison of England and the United States." *Journal of Experimental Child Psychology* 102 (3): 323–341. doi.org/10.1016/j.jecp.2008.05.008.

Ellerman, A. M., E. J. Lindo, P. Morphy, and D. L. Compton. 2009. "The Impact of Vocabulary Instruction on Passage-Level Comprehension of School-Age Children: A Meta-Analysis." *Journal of Research on Educational Effectiveness* 2 (1): 1–44. doi.org/10.1080/19345740802539200.

Engel, C., K. Lillie, S. Zurawski, and B. G. Travers. 2018. "Curriculum-Based Handwriting Programs: A Systematic Review with Effect Sizes." *The American Journal of Occupational Therapy* 72 (3): 7203205010p1–7203205010p8. doi.org/10.5014/ajot.2018.027110.

Erbeli, F., M. Rice, Y. Xu, M. E. Bishop, and J. M. Goodrich. 2024. "A Meta-Analysis on the Optimal Cumulative Dosage of Early Phonemic Awareness Instruction." *Scientific Studies of Reading* 28 (4): 345–370.

Evans, M. A., and J. Saint-Aubin. 2005. "What Children Are Looking at During Shared Storybook Reading: Evidence from Eye Movement Monitoring." *Psychological Science* 16 (11): 913–920. doi.org/10.1111/j.1467-9280.2005.01636.x.

Farrell, L., M. Hunter, and T. Osenga. "A New Model for Teaching High Frequency Words." Reading Rockets. readingrockets.org/topics/phonics-and-decoding/articles/new-model-teaching-high-frequency-words. Accessed August 4, 2024.

Farry-Thorn, M., and R. Treiman. 2022. "Prereaders' Knowledge About the Nature of Book Reading." *Reading and Writing* 35: 1933–1952.

Feng, L., A. Lindner, X. R. Ji, and R. Malatesha Joshi. 2019. "The Roles of Handwriting and Keyboarding in Writing: A Meta-Analytic Review." *Reading and Writing* 32 (1): 33–63. doi.org/10.1007/s11145-017-9749-x.

Ferlazzo, L., and K. H. Sypnieski. 2018. "Activating Prior Knowledge with English Language Learners." *Edutopia,* March 29, 2018. edutopia.org/article/activating-prior-knowledge-english-language-learners/.

Filderman, M. J., C. R. Austin, A. N., Boucher, K. O'Donnell, and E. A. Swanson. 2022. "A Meta-Analysis of the Effects of Reading Comprehension Interventions on the Reading Comprehension Outcomes of Struggling Readers in Third through 12th Grades." *Exceptional Children* 88 (2): 163–184. doi.org/10.1177/00144029211050860.

Foorman, B., N. Beyler, K. Borradaile, M. Coyne, C. A. Denton, J. Dimino, J. Furgeson, L. Hayes, J. Henke, L. Justice, B. Keating, W. Lewis, S. Sattar, A. Streke, R. Wagner, and S. Wissel. 2016. *Foundational Skills to Support Reading for Understanding in Kindergarten through 3rd Grade* (NCEE 2016-4008). National Center for Education Evaluation and Regional Assistance (NCEE), Institute of Education Sciences, U.S. Department of Education. ies.ed.gov/ncee/wwc/practiceguide/21.

Foorman, B. R., D. J. Francis, K. C. Davidson, M. W. Harm, and J. Griffin. 2004. "Variability in Text Features in Six Grade 1 Basal Reading Programs." *Scientific Studies of Reading* 8 (2): 167–197. doi.org/10.1207/s1532799xssr0802_4.

Fry, E. 1980. "The New Instant Word List." *The Reading Teacher* 34 (3): 284–289.

Geiger, A. n.d. "Syntax and Semantics in Structured Literacy." *The Measured Mom*. Accessed May 24, 2024. themeasuredmom.com syntax-and-semantics-in-structured-literacy.

Gersten, R., D. Compton, C. M. Connor, J. Dimino, L. Santoro, S. Linan-Thompson, and W. D. Till. 2008. *Assisting Students Struggling with Reading: Response to Intervention and Multi-Tier Intervention for Reading in the Primary Grades. A Practice Guide.* (NCEE 2009-4045). National Center for Education Evaluation and Regional Assistance, Institute of Education Sciences, U.S. Department of Education. ies.ed.gov/ncee/wwc/Docs/PracticeGuide/rti_reading_pg_021809.pdf.

Gersten, R. M., L. Fuchs, and S. K. Baker. 2001. "Teaching Reading Comprehension Strategies to Students with Learning Disabilities: A Review of Research." *Review of Educational Research* 71 (2): 279–320. doi.org/10.3102/00346543071002279.

Gibbons, G. 2010. *Alligators and Crocodiles.* New York: Holiday House.

Gough, P. B., and W. E. Tunmer. 1986. "Decoding, Reading, and Reading Disability." *Remedial and Special Education* 7 (1): 6–10. doi.org/10.1177/074193258600700104.

Graham, S., and K. R. Harris. 2013. "Designing an Effective Writing Program." In *Best Practices in Writing Instruction* (2nd ed.), edited by S. Graham, C. A. MacArthur, and J. Fitzgerald, 3–25. New York: Guilford.

Graham, S., and M. Hebert. 2010. *Writing to Read: Evidence for How Writing Can Improve Reading: A Report from Carnegie Corporation of New York.* Carnegie Corporation of New York Report. Washington, DC: Alliance for Excellent Education. carnegie.org/media/filer_public/9d/e2/9de20604-a055-42da-bc00-77da949b29d7/ccny_report_2010_writing.pdf.

Graham, S., D. McKeown, S. Kiuhara, and K. Harris. 2012. "A Meta-Analysis of Writing Instruction for Students in the Elementary Grades." *Journal of Educational Psychology* 104 (4): 879–896. doi.org/10.1037/a0029185.

Graham, S., and D. Perin. 2007. *Writing Next: Effective Strategies to Improve Writing of Adolescents in Middle and High Schools.* Carnegie Corporation of New York Report. Washington, DC: Alliance for Excellent Education. media.carnegie.org/filer_public/3c/f5/3cf58727-34f4-4140-a014-723a00ac56f7/ccny_report_2007_writing.pdf

Grote-Garcia, S., and E. Ortlieb. 2023. "What's Hot in Literacy: The Duality of Explicit Instruction and Cultural and Linguistic Considerations." *Literacy Research and Instruction* 62 (1): 1–15. doi.org/10.1080/19388071.2023.2162207.

Hadley, E. B., E. M. Barnes, B. M. Wiernik, and M. Raghavan. 2022. "A Meta-Analysis of Teacher Language Practices in Early Childhood Classrooms." *Early Childhood Research Quarterly* 59: 186–202. doi.org/10.1016/j.ecresq.2021.12.002.

Hadley, E. B., K. M. Newman, and J. Mock. 2020. "Setting the Stage for TALK: Strategies for Encouraging Language-Building Conversations." *The Reading Teacher* 74 (1): 39–48. doi.org/10.1002/trtr.1900.

Hebert, M., J. J. Bohaty, J. R. Nelson, and J. Brown. 2016. "The Effects of Text Structure Instruction on Expository Reading Comprehension: A Meta-Analysis." *Journal of Educational Psychology* 108 (5): 609–629. dx.doi.org/10.1037/edu0000082.

Herrera, S., B. M. Phillips, Y. Newton, J. L. Dombek, and J. A. Hernandez. 2021. *Effectiveness of Early Literacy Instruction: Summary of 20 Years of Research (REL 2021–084)*. U.S. Department of Education, Institute of Education Sciences, National Center for Education Evaluation and Regional Assistance, Regional Educational Laboratory Southeast.

Hilte, M., and P. Reitsma. 2006. "Spelling Pronunciation and Visual Preview Both Facilitate Learning to Spell Irregular Words." *Annals of Dyslexia* 56 (2): 301–318. doi.org/10.1007/s11881-006-0013-3.

Hindeman, A. H., B. A. Wasik, and D. E. Bradley. 2019. "How Classroom Conversations Unfold: Exploring Teacher-Child Exchanges During Shared Book Reading." *Early Education and Development* 30 (4): 478–495. doi.org/10.1080/10409289.2018.1556009.

Hulme, C., P. J. Hatcher, K. Nation, A. Brown, J. Adams, and G. Stuart. 2002. "Phoneme Awareness Is a Better Predictor of Early Reading Skill Than Onset-Rime Awareness." *Journal of Experimental Child Psychology* 82 (1): 2–28.

Jenkins, J. R., J. A. Peyton, E. A. Sanders, and P. F. Vadasy. 2004. "Effects of Reading Decodable Texts in Supplemental First-Grade Tutoring." *Scientific Studies of Reading* 8 (1): 53–85. doi.org/10.1207/s1532799xssr0801_4.

Jenkins, S. and R. Page. 2008. *What Do You Do with a Tail Like This?* New York: Scholastic.

Jones, C. D., and D. R. Reutzel. 2012. "Enhanced Alphabet Knowledge Instruction: Exploring a Change of Frequency, Focus, and Distributed Cycles of Review." *Reading Psychology* 33 (5): 448–464.

Juel, C., and D. Roper. 1985. "The Influence of Basal Readers on First Grade Reading." *Reading Research Quarterly* 20 (2): 134–152. doi.org/10.2307/747751.

Justice, L. M., R. P. Bowles, and L. E. Skibbe. 2006. "Measuring Preschool Attainment of Print Concept Knowledge: A Study of Typical and At-Risk 3- to 5-Year-Old Children Using Item Response Theory." *Language, Speech, and Hearing Services in Schools* 37 (3): 224–235. doi.org/10.1044/0161-1461(2006/024).

Justice, L. M., and H. K. Ezell. 2001. "Word and Print Awareness in 4-Year-old Children." *Child Language Teaching and Therapy* 17 (3): 207–225. doi.org/10.1177/026565900101700303.

Justice, L. M., and H. K. Ezell. 2002. "Use of Storybook Reading to Increase Print Awareness in At Risk Children." *American Journal of Speech-Language Pathology* 11 (1): 17–29. doi.org/10.1044/1058-0360(2002/003).

Justice, L. M., J. N. Kaderavek, X. Fan, A. Sofka, and A. Hunt. 2009. "Accelerating Preschoolers' Early Literacy Development through Classroom-Based Teacher–Child Storybook Reading and Explicit Print Referencing." *Language, Speech, and Hearing Services in Schools* 40 (1): 67–85. doi.org/10.1044/0161-1461(2008/07-0098).

Justice, L. M., A. S. McGinty, S. B. Piasta, J. N. Kaderavek, X. Fan. 2010. "Print-Focused Read-Alouds in Preschool Classrooms: Intervention Effectiveness and Moderators of Child Outcomes." *Language, Speech, and Hearing Services in Schools* 41 (4): 504–520. doi.org/10.1044/0161-1461(2010/09-0056).

Justice, L. M., L. E. Skibbe, A. Canning, and C. Lankford. 2005. "Pre-schoolers, Print and Storybooks: An Observational Study Using Eye Movement Analysis." *Journal of Research in Reading* 28 (3): 229–243. doi.org/10.1111/j.1467-9817.2005.00267.x.

Justice, L. M., and A. E. Sofka. 2013. *Engaging Children with Print: Building Early Literacy Skills through Quality Read-alouds*. New York: Guilford.

Kambach, A. E., and H.A. Mesmer. 2024. "Comprehension for Emergent Readers: Revisiting the Reading Rope." *The Reading Teacher* 77 (6): 888–898.

Kearns, D. M., H. J. Rogers, T. Koriakin, and R. Al Ghanem. 2016. "Semantic and Phonological Ability to Adjust Recoding: A Unique Correlate of Word Reading Skill?" *Scientific Studies of Reading* 20 (6): 455–470. doi.org/10.1080/10888438.2016.1217865.

Kearns, D. M., and V. M. Whaley. 2019. "Helping Students with Dyslexia Read Long Words: Using Syllables and Morphemes." *Teaching Exceptional Children* 51 (3): 212–225.

Kelly, C., S. Leitão, K. Smith-Lock, and B. Heritage. 2019. "The Effectiveness of a Classroom-Based Phonological Awareness Program for 4–5-Year-Olds." *International Journal of Speech-Language Pathology* 21 (1): 101–113. doi.org/10.1080/17549507.2017.1400589.

Kemeny, L. 2023. *7 Mighty Moves: Research-Backed, Classroom-Tested Strategies to Ensure K-to-3 Reading Success*. New York: Scholastic.

Kendeou, P., P. van den Broek, M. J. White, and J. S. Lynch. 2009. "Predicting Reading Comprehension in Early Elementary School: The Independent Contributions of Oral Language and Decoding Skills." *Journal of Educational Psychology* 101 (4): 765–778. doi.org/10.1037/a0015956.

Kenner, B. B., N. P. Terry, A. H. Friehling, and L. L Namy. 2017. "Phonemic Awareness Development in 2.5- and 3.5-Year-Old Children: An Examination of Emergent, Receptive, Knowledge, and Skills." *Reading and Writing* 30: 1575–1594. doi.org/10.1007/s11145-017-9738-0.

Klingner, J. K., S. Vaughn, M. E. Arguelles, M. Tejero Hughes, and S. Ahwee Leftwich. 2004. "Collaborative Strategic Reading: 'Real-World' Lessons from Classroom Teachers." *Remedial and Special Education* 25 (5): 291–302. doi.org/10.1177/07419325040250050301.

Kilpatrick, D.A. 2015. *Essentials of Assessing, Preventing, and Overcoming Reading Difficulties*. Hoboken, NJ: Wiley.

Kuhn, M. R., T. Rasinski, and C. Young. 2013. "Best Practices in Fluency Instruction." In *Best Practices in Literacy Instruction* (6th ed.), edited by L. M. Morrow and L. B. Gambrell, 271–288. New York: Guilford.

Kuhn, M. R., P. J. Schwanenflugel, E. B. Meisinger, B. A. Levy, and T. V. Rasinski, eds. 2010. "Aligning Theory and Assessment of Reading Fluency: Automaticity, Prosody, and Definitions of Fluency." *Reading Research Quarterly* 45 (2): 230–251. doi.org/10.1598/RRQ.45.2.4.

Kuhn, M. R., P. J. Schwanenflugel, R. D. Morris, L. M. Morrow, D. G. Woo, E. B. Meisinger, R. A. Sevcik, B. A. Bradley, and S. A. Stahl. 2006. "Teaching Children to Become Fluent and Automatic Readers." *Journal of Literacy Research* 38 (4): 357–387. doi.org/10.1207/s15548430jlr3804_1.

Liberman, A. M., and I. G. Mattingly. 1985. "The Motor Theory of Speech Perception Revised." *Cognition* 21 (1): 1–36.

Lindamood, C. H., and Lindamood, P. C. 1975. *Auditory Discrimination in Depth*. Allen, TX: DLM Teaching Resources.

Lindsey, J. B. 2022. *Reading Above the Fray: Reliable, Research-Based Routines for Developing Decoding Skills*. New York: Scholastic.

Lovett, M. W., J. C. Frijters, M. Wolf, K. A. Steinbach, R. A. Sevcik, and R. D. Morris. 2017. "Early Intervention for Children at Risk for Reading Disabilities: The Impact of Grade at Intervention and Individual Differences on Intervention Outcomes." *Journal of Educational Psychology* 109 (7): 889–914. doi:10.1037/edu0000181.

Lovett, M. W., L. Lacerenza, S. L. Borden, J. C. Frijters, K. A. Steinbach, and M. De Palma. 2000. "Components of Effective Remediation for Developmental Reading Disabilities: Combining Phonological and Strategy-Based Instruction to Improve Outcomes." *Journal of Educational Psychology* 92 (2): 263–283. doi.org/10.1037/0022-0663.92.2.263.

MacKay, E., E. Lynch, T. S. Duncan, and S. H. Deacon. 2021. "Informing the Science of Reading: Students' Awareness of Sentence-Level Information Is Important for Reading Comprehension." *Reading Research Quarterly* 56 (S1): S221–S230. doi.org/10.1002/rrq.397.

Malik, K. 2020. "Science Is Ever Evolving, Just Like the Human Race." *The Guardian*, February 16, 2020. theguardian.com/commentisfree/2020/feb/16/how-science-evolves-just-like-human-race.

Manyak, P., L. Z. Blachowicz, and M. Graves. 2021. "The Multifaceted, Comprehensive Vocabulary Instructional Program: Quantitative Findings from a Three-Year Formative Experiment." *Literacy Research and Instruction* 60 (4): 301–331. doi.10.1080/19388071.2020.1822473.

Manyak, P. C., and A.-M. Manyak. 2021. "Multi-Faceted Vocabulary Instruction in a Third-Grade Class: Findings from a Three-Year Formative Experiment." *Reading Psychology,* 42 (2): 73–110. doi.org/10.1080/02702711.2021.1878678.

Manyak, P. C., A.-M. Manyak, and E. M. Kappus. 2021. "Lessons from a Decade of Research on Multifaceted Vocabulary Instruction." *The Reading Teacher* 75 (1): 27–39. doi.org/10.1002/trtr.2010.

McGuinness, D. 1997. *Why Our Children Can't Read, and What We Can Do about It: A Scientific Revolution in Reading*. New York: Simon & Schuster.

Melby-Lervåg, M., and C. Hulme. 2013. "Is Working Memory Training Effective? A Meta-Analytic Review." *Developmental Psychology* 49 (2): 270–291. doi.org/10.1037/a0028228.

Mesmer, H. A. E. 2008. *Tools for Matching Readers to Texts: Research-Based Practices*. New York: Guilford.

Mesmer, H. A. E., and K. Lake. 2010. "The Role of Syllable Awareness and Syllable-Controlled Text in the Development of Finger-Point Reading." *Reading Psychology* 31 (2): 176–201.

Mesmer, H. A., and T. O. Williams. 2015. "Examining the Role of Syllable Awareness in a Model of Concept of Word: Findings from Preschoolers." *Reading Research Quarterly* 50 (4): 483–497.

Møller, H. L., J. O. Mortensen, and C. Elbro. 2022. "Effects of Integrated Spelling in Phonics Instruction for At-Risk Children in Kindergarten." *Reading & Writing Quarterly* 38 (1): 67–82.

Morris, D., J. W. Bloodgood, R. G. Lomax, and J. Perney. 2003. "Developmental Steps in Learning to Read: A Longitudinal Study in Kindergarten and First Grade." *Reading Research Quarterly* 38 (3): 302–328. doi.org/10.1598/RRQ.38.3.1.

Muter, V., C. Hulme, M. Snowling, and S. Taylor. 1998. "Segmentation, Not Rhyming, Predicts Early Progress in Learning to Read." *Journal of Experimental Child Psychology* 71 (1): 3–27.

Nation, K., P. Angell, and A. Castles. 2007. "Orthographic Learning via Self-Teaching in Children Learning to Read English: Effects of Exposure, Durability, and Context." *Journal of Experimental Child Psychology* 96 (1): 71–84.

Nation, K., and C. Hulme. 1997. "Phonemic Segmentation, Not Onset-Rime Segmentation, Predicts Early Reading and Spelling Skills." *Reading Research Quarterly* 32 (2): 154-167. doi.org/10.1598/RRQ.32.2.2.

National Center on Improving Literacy. 2023. *The Educator's Science of Reading Toolbox: Explicit Vocabulary Instruction to Build Equitable Access for All Learners*. Washington, DC: U.S. Department of Education, Office of Elementary and Secondary Education, Office of Special Education Programs, National Center on Improving Literacy. improvingliteracy.org/code-assets/briefs/explicit-vocabulary-instruction.pdf.

National Early Literacy Panel. 2008. *Developing Early Literacy: Report of the National Early Literacy Panel: A Scientific Synthesis of Early Literacy Development and Implications for Intervention*. National Institute for Literacy, National Center for Family Literacy. nichd.nih.gov/sites/default/files/publications/pubs/documents/NELPReport09.pdf.

National Institute of Child Health and Human Development, National Institute of Health, and Department of Health and Human Services. 2000. *Report of the National Reading Panel: Teaching Children to Read: Reports of the Subgroups* (00-4754). U.S. Government Printing Office.

Nevo, E., and V. Vaknin-Nusbaum. 2018. "Enhancing Language and Print-Concept Skills by Using Interactive Storybook Reading in Kindergarten." *Journal of Early Childhood Literacy* 18 (4): 545–569.

O'Connor, R. E., K. D. Beach, V. M. Sanchez, K. M. Bocian, and L. J. Flynn. 2015. "Building BRIDGES: A Design Experiment to Improve Reading and United States History Knowledge of Poor Readers in Eighth Grade." *Exceptional Children* 81 (4) 399–425. doi.org/10.1177/0014402914563706.

O'Connor, R. E., K. M. Bell, K. R. Harty, L. K. Larkin, S. M. Sackor, and N. Zigmond. 2002. "Teaching Reading to Poor Readers in the Intermediate Grades: A Comparison of Text Difficulty." *Journal of Educational Psychology* 94 (3): 474–485. doi.org/10.1037/0022-0663.94.3.474.

O'Connor, R. E., H. L. Swanson, and C. Geraghty. 2010. "Improvement in Reading Rate Under Independent and Difficult Text Levels: Influences on Word and Comprehension Skills." *Journal of Educational Psychology* 102 (1): 1–19. doi.org/10.1037/a0017488.

O'Connor, R. E., A. White, and H. L. Swanson. 2007. "Repeated Reading versus Continuous Reading: Influences on Reading Fluency and Comprehension." *Exceptional Children* 74 (1): 31–46. doi.org/10.1177/001440290707400102.

Ouellette, G., and M. Sénéchal. 2008. "Pathways to Literacy: A Study of Invented Spelling and Its Role in Learning to Read." *Child Development* 79 (4): 899–913.

Ouellette, G., M. Sénéchal, and A. Haley. 2013. "Guiding Children's Invented Spellings: A Gateway into Literacy Learning." *The Journal of Experimental Education* 81 (2): 261–279.

Palincsar, A. S., and A. L. Brown. 1984. "Reciprocal Teaching of Comprehension-Fostering and Comprehension-Monitoring Activities." *Cognition and Instruction* 1 (2): 117–175. doi.org/10.1207/s1532690xci0102_1.

Peng, P. 2023. "The Role of Executive Function in Reading Development and Reading Intervention." *Mind, Brain, and Education* 17 (4): 246–256. doi.org/10.1111/mbe.12375.

Peng, P., and D. Fuchs. 2017. "A Randomized Control Trial of Working Memory Training with and without Strategy Instruction: Effects on Young Children's Working Memory and Comprehension." *Journal of Learning Disabilities* 50 (1): 62–80. doi.org/10.1177/0022219415594609.

Peng, P., W. Wang, M. J. Filderman, W. Zhang, and L. Lin. 2023. "The Active Ingredient in Reading Comprehension Strategy Intervention for Struggling Readers: A Bayeseian Network Meta-analysis." *Review of Educational Research* 94 (2): 228–267. doi.org/10.3102/00346543231171345.

Perfetti, C. A., I. Beck, L. C. Bell, and C. Hughes. 1987. "Phonemic Knowledge and Learning to Read Are Reciprocal: A Longitudinal Study of First Grade Children." *Merrill-Palmer Quarterly* 33 (3): 283–319.

Phillips, B. M. 2023. "Language Interventions in Early Childhood: Summary and Implications from a Multistudy Program of Research." In *Handbook on the Science of Early Literacy*, edited by S. Neuman, S. Q. Cabell, and N. P. Terry, 139–150. New York: Guilford.

Phillips, B. M., S. B. Piasta, J. L. Anthony, C. J. Lonigan, D. J. Francis. 2012. "IRTs of the ABCs: Children's Letter Name Acquisition." *Journal of School Psychology* 50 (4): 461–481. doi.org/10.1016/j.jsp.2012.05.002.

Piasta, S. B., D. J. Purpura, and R. K. Wagner. 2010. "Fostering Alphabet Knowledge Development: A Comparison of Two Instructional Approaches." *Reading and Writing: An Interdisciplinary Journal* 23 (6): 607–626. doi.org/10.1007/s11145-009-9174-x.

Pressley, M., and P. Afflerbach. 1995. *Verbal Protocols of Reading: The Nature of Constructively Responsive Reading* (1st ed.). New York: Routledge. doi.org/10.4324/9780203052938.

Pressley, M., and P. B. El-Dinary. 1997. "What We Know About Translating Comprehension Strategies Instruction Research into Practice." *Journal of Learning Disabilities* 30 (5): 486–488. doi.org/10.1177/002221949703000504.

Pritchard, V. E., S. A. Malone, and C. Hulme. 2021. "Early Handwriting Ability Predicts the Growth of Children's Spelling, but Not Reading, Skills." *Scientific Studies of Reading* 25 (4): 304–331 doi.org/10.1080/10888438.2020.1778705.

Pugh, A., D. M. Kearns, and E. H. Hiebert. 2023. "Text Types and Their Relation to Efficacy in Beginning Reading Interventions." *Reading Research Quarterly* 58 (4): 710–732. doi.org/10.1002/rrq.513.

Puzio, K., G. T. Colby, and D. Algeo-Nichols. 2020. "Differentiated Literacy Instruction: Boondoggle or Best Practice?" *Review of Educational Research* 90 (4): 459–498. doi.org/10.3102/0034654320933536.

Pyle, N., A. C. Vasquez, B. Lignugaris/Kraft, S. L. Gillam, D. R. Reutzel, A. Olszewski, H. Segura, D. Hartzheim, W. Laing, and D. Pyle. 2017. "Effects of Expository Text Structure Interventions on Comprehension: A Meta-Analysis." *Reading Research Quarterly* 52 (4): 469–501. doi.org/10.1002/rrq.179.

Ray, K., K. Dally, K. Colyvas, and A. E. Lane. 2021. "The Effects of a Whole-Class Kindergarten Handwriting Intervention on Early Reading Skills." *Reading Research Quarterly* 56 (S1): S193–S207. doi.org/10.1002/rrq.395.

Reading League. n.d. "What Is the Science of Reading?" Accessed August 12, 2024. thereadingleague.org/what-is-the-science-of-reading/.

REL West. 2021. *Effect Size Basics: Understanding the Strength of a Program's Impact*. WestEd. wested.org/resources/rel-west-effect-size-basics-infographic.

Reitsma, P. 1983. "Printed Word Learning in Beginning Readers." *Journal of Experimental Child Psychology* 36 (2): 321–339.

Reutzel, D. R., J. A. Smith, and P. C. Fawson. 2005. "An Evaluation of Two Approaches for Teaching Reading Comprehension Strategies in the Primary Years Using Science Information Texts." *Early Childhood Research Quarterly* 20 (3): 276–305. doi.org/10.1016/j.ecresq.2005.07.002.

Robbins, H. H., and K. Hilden. 2016. "Teaching Text Structures to Support Content-Area Reading and Writing." *Reading in Virginia* 38: 41–50.

Roberts, T. A. 2005. "Articulation Accuracy and Vocabulary Size Contributions to Phonemic Awareness and Word Reading in English Language Learners." *Journal of Educational Psychology* 97 (4): 601–616. doi.org/10.1037/0022-0663.97.4.601.

Roberts, T. A. 2021. "Learning Letters: Evidence and Questions from a Science-of-Reading Perspective." *Reading Research Quarterly* 56: S171–S192.

Roberts, T. A., P. F. Vadasy, and E. A. Sanders. 2018. "Preschoolers' Alphabet Learning: Letter Name and Sound Instruction, Cognitive Processes, and English Proficiency." *Early Childhood Research Quarterly* 44: 257–274. doi.org/10.1016/j.ecresq.2018.04.011.

Roehling, J. V., M. Hebert, J. R. Nelson, and J. J. Bohaty. 2017. "Text Structure Strategies for Improving Expository Reading Comprehension." *The Reading Teacher* 71 (1): 71–82. doi.org/10.1002/trtr.1590.

Saha, N. M., L. E. Cutting, S. Del Tufo, and S. Bailey. 2021. "Initial Validation of a Measure of Decoding Difficulty as a Unique Predictor of Miscues and Passage Reading Fluency." *Reading and Writing* 34 (2): 497–527. doi.org/10.1007/s11145-020-10073-x.

Santangelo, T., and S. Graham. 2016. "A Comprehensive Meta-Analysis of Handwriting Instruction." *Educational Psychology Review* 28 (2): 225–265. doi.org/10.1007/s10648-015-9335-1.

Savage, R., G. Georgiou, R. Parrila and K. Maiorino. 2018. "Preventative Reading Interventions Teaching Direct Mapping of Graphemes in Texts and Set-for-Variability Aid At-Risk Learners." *Scientific Studies of Reading* 22 (3): 225–247.

Scarborough, H. S. 2001. "Connecting Early Language and Literacy to Later Reading (Dis)abilities: Evidence, Theory, and Practice." In *Handbook of Early Literacy Research* (Vol. 1), edited by S. B. Neuman and D. K. Dickinson, 97–110. New York: Guilford.

Schwanenflugel, P. J., A. M. Hamilton, J. M. Wisenbaker, M. R. Kuhn, and S. A. Stahl. 2004. "Becoming a Fluent Reader: Reading Skill and Prosodic Features in the Oral Reading of Young Readers." *Journal of Educational Psychology* 96 (1): 119–129. doi.org/10.1037/0022-0663.96.1.119.

Scott, C. M., and C. Balthazar. 2013. "The Role of Complex Sentence Knowledge in Children with Reading and Writing Difficulties." *Perspectives on Language and Literacy* 39 (3): 18–30.

Sedita, J. 2020a. "Syntactic Awareness: Teaching Sentence Structure (Part 1)." *The Keys to Literacy Blog*, June 2, 2020. keystoliteracy.com/blog/syntactic-awareness-teaching-sentence-structure-part-1/.

Sedita, J. 2020b. "What Are Cohesive Devices and How Do They Affect Comprehension?" *The Keys to Literacy Blog*, August 19, 2020. keystoliteracy.com/blog/what-are-cohesive-devices-and-how-do-they-affect-comprehension/.

Sénéchal, M., G. Ouellette, and H. N. L. Nguyen. 2023. "Invented Spelling: An Integrative Review of Descriptive, Correlational, and Causal Evidence." In *Handbook on the Science of Early Literacy*, edited by S. Q. Cabell, S. B. Neuman, and N. P. Terry, 95–106. New York: Guilford.

Shanahan, T. 2020. "What Constitutes a Science of Reading Instruction?" *Reading Research Quarterly* 55 (1): S235–S247. doi.org/10.1002/rrq.349.

Share, D. L. 1995. "Phonological Recoding and Self-Teaching: *Sine qua non* of Reading Acquisition." *Cognition* 55 (2): 151–218. doi.org/10.1016/0010-0277(94)00645-2.

Share, D. L. 2004. "Knowing Letter Names and Learning Sounds: A Causal Connection." *Journal of Experimental Child Psychology* 88 (3): 213–233. doi.org/10.1016/j.jecp.2004.03.005.

Silverman, R. D., E. Johnson, K. Keane, and S. Khanna. 2020. "Beyond Decoding: A Meta-Analysis of the Effects of Language Comprehension Interventions on K–5 Students' Language and Literacy Outcomes." *Reading Research Quarterly* 55 (S1): S207–S233. doi.org/10.1002/rrq.346.

Stahl, K. 2004. "Proof, Practice, and Promise: Comprehension Strategy Instruction in the Primary Grades." *The Reading Teacher* 57 (7): 598–609.

Stahl, S. A. 1998. "Understanding Shifts in Reading and Its Instruction." *Peabody Journal of Education* 73 (3-4): 31–67. doi.org/10.1080/0161956X.1998.9681885.

Stahl, S. A., and K. Heubach. 2005. "Fluency-Oriented Reading Instruction." *Journal of Literacy Research* 37 (1): 25–60. doi.org/10.1207/s15548430jlr3701_2.

Stahl, S. A., and B. A. Murray. 1994. "Defining Phonological Awareness and Its Relationship to Early Reading." *Journal of Educational Psychology* 86 (2): 221–234. doi.org/10.1037/0022-0663.86.2.221.

Stanovich, K. E. 1980. "Toward an Interactive-Compensatory Model of Individual Differences in the Development of Reading Fluency." *Reading Research Quarterly* 16 (1): 32–71.

Steacy, L. M., D. Fuchs, J. K. Gilbert, D. M. Kearns, A. M. Elleman, and A. A. Edwards. 2020. "Sight Word Acquisition in First Grade Students at Risk for Reading Disabilities: An Item-Level Exploration of the Number of Exposures Required for Mastery." *Annals of Dyslexia* 70 (2): 259–274. doi.org/10.1007/s11881-020-00198-7.

Sunde, K., B. Furnes, and K. Lundetræ. 2020. "Does Introducing the Letters Faster Boost the Development of Children's Letter Knowledge, Word Reading and Spelling in the First Year of School?" *Scientific Studies of Reading* 24 (2): 141–158. doi.org/10.1080/10888438.2019.1615491.

Treiman, R. 2000. "The Foundations of Literacy." *Current Directions in Psychological Science* 9 (3): 89–92. doi.org/10.1111/1467-8721.00067.

Treiman, R., B. F. Pennington, L. Shriberg, and R. Boada. 2008. "Which Children Benefit from Letter Names in Learning Letter Sounds?" *Cognition* 106 (3): 1322–1338. doi.org/10.1016/j.cognition.2007.06.006.

Treiman, R., L. Sotak, and M. Bowman. 2001. "The Roles of Letter Names and Letter Sounds in Connecting Print and Speech." *Memory & Cognition* 29 (6): 860–873. doi.org/10.3758/BF03196415.

Truss, L., and B. Timmons. 2006. *Eats, Shoots & Leaves: Why, Commas Really Do Make a Difference!* New York: G. P. Putnam's Sons Books for Young Readers.

Treptow, M. A., M. K. Burns, and J. J. McComas. 2007. "Reading at the Frustration, Instructional, and Independent Levels: The Effects on Students' Reading Comprehension and Time on Task." *School Psychology Review* 36 (1): 159–166.

Vadasy, P. F., and E. A. Sanders. 2009. "Supplemental Fluency Intervention and Determinants of Reading Outcomes." *Scientific Studies of Reading* 13 (5): 383–425. doi.org/10.1080/10888430903162894.

Vadasy, P. F., and E. A. Sanders. 2021. "Introducing Grapheme-Phoneme Correspondences (GPCs): Exploring Rate and Complexity in Phonics Instruction for Kindergartners with Limited Literacy Skills." *Reading and Writing* 34: 109–138. doi.org/10.1007/s11145-020-10064-y.

Vadasy, P. F., E. A. Sanders, and J. A. Peyton. 2005. "Relative Effectiveness of Reading Practice or Word-Level Instruction in Supplemental Tutoring: How Text Matters." *Journal of Learning Disabilities* 38 (4): 364–380.

Vadasy, P. F., E. A. Sanders, J. A. Peyton, and J. R. Jenkins. 2002. "Timing and Intensity of Tutoring: A Closer Look at the Conditions for Effective Early Literacy Tutoring." *Learning Disabilities Research and Practice* 17 (4): 227–241. doi.org/10.1111/1540-5826.00048.

Vadasy, P. F., E. A. Sanders, and S. Tudor. 2007. "Effectiveness of Paraeducator-Supplemented Individual Instruction: Beyond Basic Decoding Skills." *Journal of Learning Disabilities* 40 (6): 508–525.

Vygotsky, L. S. 1986 [1934]. *Thought and Language*, edited by A. Kozulin, translated by E. Hanfmann and G. Vakar. Cambridge, MA: MIT Press.

Wasik, B. A., and C. Iannone-Campbell. 2012. "Developing Vocabulary Through Purposeful, Strategic Conversations." *The Reading Teacher* 66 (4): 321–332. doi.org/10.1002/TRTR.01095.

Wijekumar, K., B. J. F. Meyer, P.-W. Lei, A. C. Hernandez, and D. L. August. 2018. "Improving Content Area Reading Comprehension of Spanish Speaking English Learners in Grades 4 and 5 Using Web-Based Text Structure Instruction." *Reading and Writing* 31 (9): 1969–1996. doi.org/10.1007/s11145-017-9802-9.

Williams, J. P., K. M. Hall, K. D. Lauer, K. B. Stafford, L. A. DeSisto, and J. S. deCani. 2005. "Expository Text Comprehension in the Primary Grade Classroom." *Journal of Educational Psychology* 97 (4): 538–550. doi.org/10.1037/0022-0663.97.4.538.

Williams, J. P., J. C. Kao, L. S. Pao, J. G. Ordynans, J. G. Atkins, R. Jheng, and D. DeBonis. 2016. "Close Analysis of Texts with Structure (CATS): An Intervention to Teach Reading Comprehension to At-Risk Second Graders." *Journal of Educational Psychology* 108 (8): 1061–1077. doi.org/10.1037/edu0000117.

Willingham, D. T. 2006. "The Usefulness of Brief Instruction in Reading Comprehension Strategies." *American Educator* 30 (4): 39–50.

Wright, T. S., and G. N. Cervetti. 2017. "A Systematic Review of the Research on Vocabulary Instruction That Impacts Text Comprehension." *Reading Research Quarterly* 52 (2): 203–226. doi.org/10.1002/rrq.163.

Wu, Y., L. A. Barquero, S. E. Pickren, A. T. Barber, and L. E. Cutting. 2020. "The Relationship Between Cognitive Skills and Reading Comprehension of Narrative and Expository Texts: A Longitudinal Study from Grade 1 to Grade 4." *Learning and Individual Differences* 80: 101848. doi.org/10.1016/j.lindif.2020.101848.

Yopp, H. K. 1992. "Developing Phonemic Awareness in Young Children." *The Reading Teacher* 45 (9): 696–703.

Young, C., D. Paige, and T. V. Rasinski. 2022. *Artfully Teaching the Science of Reading*. New York: Routledge.

Zhang, Z., and P. Peng. 2023. "Longitudinal Reciprocal Relations Among Reading, Executive Function, and Social-Emotional Skills: Maybe Not for All." *Journal of Educational Psychology* 115 (3): 475–501. doi.org/10.1037/edu0000787.

Zheng, H., X. Miao, Y. Dong, and D.-C. Yuan. 2023. "The Relationship between Grammatical Knowledge and Reading Comprehension: A Meta-Analysis." *Frontiers in Psychology* 14: 1098568. doi.org/10.3389/fpsyg.2023.1098568.

Zutell, J., and T. V. Rasinski. 1991. "Training Teachers to Attend to Their Students' Oral Reading Fluency." *Theory into Practice* 30 (3): 211–217.

Index

A

accountable spelling, 82
acrophonic letters, 23–24, 25, 26
Actions for the Classroom. *See* instructional recommendations (So What?)
active self-regulation, 9–10
Active View of Reading, 9–10, 107, 161
After the Fall (Santat), 119, 121
Alligators and Crocodiles (Gibbons), 123, 148
alphabet chart, 85
alphabetic knowledge/instruction, 17. *See also* letter(s) and letter instruction
    articulatory pictures/mouth moves and, 50–51
    concept of word in print and, 31–32, 33
    handwriting and, 92, 93
    sight-word learning and, 74–75
    alphabetic principle, invented spelling and, 81, 84
anchor charts, 49, 54, 124, 140, 148
Arnold, Ted, 158
articulatory gestures (mouth moves), 49–54
Articulatory Learning (AL), 51
articulatory pictures, 50–54
assessment
    of cognitive flexibility, 156–158
    Enhanced Alphabet Knowledge (EAK), 20
    high-frequency words and, 71
    invented spellings and, 85
    letter instruction and, 21, 22
    meta-analysis and, 6
    of oral reading fluency/prosody, 106, 108, 110
    self-assessment of teacher talk, 164–165
    of sentence comprehension, 149
    vocabulary, 116

at-risk students. *See also* multilingual learners
    letter instruction for, 19, 20–21
    number of letters to teach per week, 22
    text-structure instruction and, 138

B

background knowledge, 8, 10–11, 131, 132, 162
basal programs, 123, 127
basal reader, 58
beginning readers
    highly decodable texts and, 55, 60, 61
    phonological awareness skills of, 43
    reader-text matching and, 173–174
    sensitive to text difficulty, 172
    text difficulty and, 170
blending sounds, 43, 45–46
books, matching reading-levels to, 169–175
Bridging Language, 163
bridging processes, in Active View of Reading, 9–10

C

Cartwright, Kelly, 157
cause and effect text structure, 135, 136
caveats and cautions, 11
    on comprehension strategies, 128, 132–133
    on decodable texts, 61
    on executive function and cognitive flexibility, 158
    on handwriting instruction, 94
    on invented spelling, 86
    on letter introduction, 20
    on number of times to present specific words, 68–69
    on reading with expression/prosody, 109
    on sentence comprehension, 150
    on teaching expository text structure, 142
    on text difficulty and prosody, 109
    on text-structure instruction, 142
    on vocabulary instruction/knowledge, 118
Clay, Marie, 29
close-ended questions, 163
cloze tasks, 147, 172
clue words, 139
code instruction, handwriting instruction and, 93
cognitive flexibility, 154–155, 156–159
cohesive ties, teaching, 147–148, 150
Collaborative Strategic Reading, 124
comparison text structure, 135, 136, 138–139
compound words, 158
comprehension strategies, 3
    background knowledge and, 131–132
    basal programs, 123, 127
    choosing strategies to focus on, 129–133
    multi-strategy approaches, 124, 125–127
    number of strategies used and, 130–131
    overview, 123–124
    prior/background knowledge and, 129–130, 131–132, 133
    research findings on, 125–126, 130–131
    research studies on, 125, 130
    resources on, 128, 133
    single-strategy approach, 124, 125, 126

195

student opportunities for integrating strategies, 126–127
computer-based tutoring programs, 139
concept of word in print, 29–38
consolidated alphabetic stage, 74, 75
context clues, 115, 116, 118, 149
continuous reading, 100, 102
correlational studies, 3, 5, 162
counters, 43, 45, 46
cue words/phrases, 123, 135, 139
cultural knowledge, 10
cycle diagrams, 141

D

decodability, 56, 57
    highly decodable texts, 56, 57–58, 59–61, 170
    text difficulty and, 171–172
decoding
    concept of word in print and, 29, 32
    definition, 8
    learning words and number of times, 63–70
    phonemic segmentation and, 43–44, 45–46, 47
    phonological awareness and, 42
    in Scarborough's Rope model, 8
    Simple View of Reading on, 8
    and teaching print concepts, 29
    text difficulty and, 171
Denmark, research conducted in, 83
descriptive text structure, 135, 136, 139–140
diagrams, text-structure instruction and, 141
distributed review cycles, for letter instruction, 20, 21, 22
Dolch words, 77
drilling high-frequency words, 75
dual-language learners. *See* multilingual learners
Dutch children, study conducted with, 65
Dynamic Indicators of Basic Early Literacy Skills (DIBELS), 20

E

early reading-disabled (ERD) students, 73
Eats, Shoots & Leaves (Truss), 145, 151
Elkonin boxes, 40, 45
Emergent Academic Language, 163
empirical research, 3, 31

England, learning of letter sounds in, 26
Enhanced Alphabet Knowledge (EAK) instruction, 20
ESHALOV techniques, 117, 118
Even More Parts (Arnold), 158
executive functioning, 153–159
Executive Skills and Reading Comprehension: A Guide for Educators (Cartwright), 157
experimental studies, 3–4
    on articulatory gestures/mouth moves, 50–51
    on comprehension strategies, 125
    on learning letter names and sounds, 26
    on letter instruction, 50–51
    number of graphemes learner per week, 19
    on rates of letter instruction, 19
    on text difficulty, 171
explicit instruction
    phonics, 57, 59, 67
    of sentence comprehension, 145–151
    of syntax and grammar instruction, 145
    for text structure instruction, 139
    vocabulary, 113, 114, 116, 117, 119, 121
expository text structures, 135–143
expression, on Multidimensional Fluency Scale, 109
expression, reading with, 105–111

F

fine-motor skills, handwriting instruction and, 90, 91, 94
flow diagrams, 141
fluency. *See* reading fluency
fluency, handwriting and, 90, 91
Fluency-Oriented Reading Instruction (FORI), 100–101, 102, 103, 104
Four Corners technique, 131–132
full alphabetic stage, 60, 74, 75
function words, 79

G

Gates-MacGinitie Reading Tests Vocabulary Subtests, 116
generic fine-motor instruction, 91
genre knowledge, text-structure instruction and, 140
Gibbons, Gail, 123, 148
grade levels

reader-text matching and, 169, 173
    syntactic complexity and, 147
grammar instruction, 145–152
grapheme(s)
    articulatory pictures and, 52, 53
    decodability and, 57
    definition, 18
    number to introduce each week, 19
    reader-text matching and, 174
    text difficulty and, 170
grapheme-phoneme correspondences (GPCs), 55, 74, 82
graphic organizers, 124
graphophonological-semantic cognitive flexibility (GSF), 10, 155, 156, 159
Gray Oral Reading Test, 101
guiding questions, on expository text structures, 136, 140

H

Handbook of the Science of Early Literacy, 82–83
hand motions, 45, 46
handwriting instruction, 89–95
Head Start classrooms, read-alouds recorded in, 163
Head Start Early Learning Outcomes, 27
high-frequency words
    definition, 72
    grouped by grade, 77
    grouped by spelling pattern, 78
    highly decodable texts including, 55, 56, 58, 59
    reader-text matching and, 170
    teaching, 71–79
high-level questions, 164
highly decodable texts, 56, 57–58, 59–61, 170

I

idioms, 158, 159
IES Practice Guide for Foundational Skills, 102
inhibition, executive functioning and, 154
instructional recommendations (So What?), 11, 13
    on articulatory pictures and mouth moves, 52–54
    on comprehension strategies, 126–127, 131–133
    on decodable texts, 59–60

on executive function and cognitive flexibility, 157–159
on expository text structures, 139–142
on handwriting instruction, 93–94
on how many letters to teach per week, 20–22
on invented spelling, 84–86
on oral language development, 163–165
on oral reading practice, 102–103
on phonemic/phonological awareness, 44–47
on reader-text matching, 173–174
on reading with expression/prosody, 108–109, 110
on repeated reading and wide reading, 102–103
on sentence comprehension, 147–149, 150–151
on teaching high-frequency words, 75–79
on teaching letter names and sounds, 27–28
on teaching print concepts, 34–37
on text structure instruction, 139–141, 142
on vocabulary instruction/knowledge, 116–119
on word learning, 67–68
interactive reading, learning print concepts, 34
interactive talk, 125, 163–165
intonation, 105, 106, 107
invented spelling, 7, 81–87
irregular/less-regular words, 57, 72, 73, 74, 75

L

language comprehension. *See also* oral language development; reading comprehension
   in Active View of Reading, 9–10
   multiple factors of, 161–162
   in Simple View of Reading, 8–9
language structures, 9, 162
late reading-disabled (LRD) students, 73
Learning Strategies Curriculum, 124
lesson-to-text-match, 55
less-regular words. *See* irregular/less-regular words
letter-a-day pacing, letter instruction using, 20

letter(s) and letter instruction. *See also* alphabetic knowledge/instruction
   acrophonic, 23–24, 25, 26
   articulatory pictures and, 52–53
   coupling phonemic awareness with, 27–28, 42, 45
   definition, 18
   Enhanced Alphabet Knowledge (EAK), 20
   handwriting instruction contributing to, 92
   integrating oral phonemic awareness actions with, 46
   invented spelling and, 83, 84–85
   "letter of the week" method of teaching, 17
   number to introduce/teach per week, 17–22
   phonemic awareness instruction paired with, 42, 47
   and print referencing, 35
   teaching letter sounds *versus* letter names, 23–28
   understanding between words, sentences and, 34
   writing from memory, 93
letter cards, 52, 83
letter names, teaching, 23–28
Letter Naming Fluency, 20
letter-sound instruction, mispronunciation correction and, 74
letter-sound recognition
   handwriting instruction contributing to, 92
   invented spelling and, 83
letter sounds
   concept of word in print and, 33, 36
   focus on, for word learning, 67
   learned before decoding words, 32
   learning and teaching, 23–28
   learning high-frequency words and, 75
   orthographic mapping and, 75
   partial alphabetic stage and, 75
   phonemic awareness instruction and, 45
   self-teaching hypothesis and knowledge of, 64
letters plus articulatory pictures (LPA) instruction, 51, 52
literacy knowledge, 9, 162
logical spelling, 82

loudness, reading aloud and, 106

M

meta-analyses, 3, 6
   on comprehension strategies, 130, 131, 132
   on decodable texts, 58
   example, 7
   on handwriting instruction, 91
   on invented spellings, 83
   on language comprehension interventions, 162
   on phonemic awareness instruction, 42
   on syntax knowledge, 147
   on text-structure instruction, 137, 138–139
   on types teacher talk, 163
   on vocabulary instruction, 113, 114, 116
metaphors, 158, 159
mirrors, 51, 54
mispronunciation of words, 72, 74, 76
modeling
   for comprehension strategies, 124, 125
   in Fluency-Oriented Reading Instruction (FORI), 100, 101
   handwriting, 91, 93
   how to spell a word, 85
   how to use paragraph frames, 140
   teaching print concepts by, 34, 35, 36, 37
   when teaching sentence combining and reduction, 148–149, 151
More Parts (Arnold), 158
morphological awareness, 9, 10
Mosaic of Thought, 124
motor theory of speech perception, 50
mouth moves (articulatory gestures), 49–54
Multidimensional Fluency Scale, 108–109
Multifaceted Comprehensive Vocabulary Instruction Program (MCVIP), 115, 116, 118
multilingual learners
   articulatory instruction and, 51, 52, 53
   high-frequency word lists for, 75
   learning sight words, 75
   letter instruction for, 20–21
   letter introduction for, 19

N

number of letters to teach per week, 19–20, 22
oral language development and, 161
text-structure instruction for, 138

National Early Literacy Panel report, 42
Norway, study on letter instruction in, 19–20

O

occupational therapists, 91, 92, 93–94
online instruction, for text structure, 138, 139
open-ended questions, 163–164, 165
oral language development, 161–167
oral phonemic awareness actions, 45, 46
oral reading
    prosody and, 105–110
    repeated, 99–104
orthographic complexity scale, 171
Orthographic Learning (OL), 51
orthographic mapping, 63, 64, 66, 74–75, 76

P

pace, on Multidimensional Fluency Scale, 109
Paired Associated Learning (PAL), 50–51
paragraph frames, 123, 135, 136, 140
paraphrasing sentences, 149, 151
parent-child language, correlational studies and, 5
partial alphabetic stage, 74, 75
pausing, when reading aloud, 106, 107
Peabody Picture Vocabulary Test-Third Edition (PPVT-III), 100
Peeling Off technique, 117, 118
pencil, showing students how to hold a, 91, 93
phoneme(s). *See also* phonemic awareness
    articulatory pictures and, 52, 53
    concept of word in print and, 33
    decodability and, 57
    definition, 18
    detection of in young children, 43
phoneme deletion, 46

phoneme-grapheme correspondences. *See* grapheme-phoneme correspondences (GPCs)
phoneme-grapheme pattern, 76, 81
phoneme substitution, 46
phonemic awareness, 8
    articulatory pictures and mouth moves impacting, 51, 52
    coupling letter instruction with, 27–28, 39, 42, 47
    explained, 40
    instructional recommendations for, 44–46
    invented spellings and, 83, 85
    learning letter names/sounds and, 25–26
    mouth moves and, 51
    quantity of instruction, 44, 47
    research findings on, 41–44
    research studies on, 41
    tasks developing, 40
    teaching, 44–47
phonemic segmentation, 43, 45–46, 47, 51, 52
phonetic spelling, 82
phonics instruction
    adding mouth moves for, 53
    decodable texts and, 55, 57, 58, 59, 60
    Science of Reading (SoR) interpreted as, 2
    self-teaching and, 68
    teaching high-frequency words alongside, 75–76
phonological awareness, 8, 9, 39–47, 84, 146
phonological spelling, 82
phrasing, on Multidimensional Fluency Scale, 108, 109
picture books, 31
pictures, articulatory. *See* articulatory pictures
pitch, of the voice, 106, 107
pointing to pictures, 43
pointing to words, 36–37
polysemous words, 158, 159
pre-alphabetic stage, 32, 74–75
print concepts, 10, 29–38
print meaning, 35
print organization, 35
print referencing, 33, 35
print tracking, 36–37, 59
problem and solution text structure, 135, 136
productive tasks, 40, 43
pronunciation of words. *See* mispronunciation of words
prosody, 105–111

pseudowords, 63, 64, 65, 66, 69

Q

quantitative studies, 3
quasi-experimental studies, 6, 171
    on reader-text matching, 171
    on text difficulty and accuracy, 171
questions
    closed-ended, during read-alouds, 163
    oral language development and high-level, 164
    oral language development and open-ended, 161, 163–164, 165
    providing inspiration for anchor charts, 148
    related to print concepts, 35
    related to text structures, 136, 140

R

readability formulas, 170
read-alouds
    cohesive ties taught with, 147
    self-assessment of teacher talk during, 164–165
    teacher talk and students' vocabulary in, 163
    text difficulty and fluency during, 171–172
reader-text matching, 169–175
reading
    with expression, 105–111
    relationship between executive function and, 156
    repeated oral, 99–104
    theories on, 8–10
reading comprehension. *See also* comprehension strategies
    cognitive flexibility and, 156–157
    multiple factors of, 161–162
    prosody and, 106, 107–108
    research on interventions for, 162
    Scarborough's Rope model on, 8–9
    syntactic knowledge and, 146–147
    text difficulty and, 171, 172
    vocabulary knowledge and, 113
    wide reading and repeated reading impacting, 101

reading difficulties, students with. *See also* at-risk students; struggling readers
   complex sentence comprehension and, 149
   importance of teaching vocabulary to, 115
   teaching comprehension strategies to, 130–131
reading fluency
   in Active View of Reading, 10
   decodability and, 57, 59
   Multidimensional Fluency Scale, 108, 109
   prosody and, 107, 108
   reader-text matching and, 173–174
   text difficulty and, 171–172, 174
   wide reading and repeated reading impacting, 101, 102
Reading in the Brain (Dehaene), 23
Reading League, 2
reading level, matching text to, 169–175
receptive tasks, 40, 43
Reciprocal Teaching, 124, 132
repeated oral reading, 99–104
research. *See also* Science of Reading (SoR)
   about, 2–3
   analyzing and comparing studies, 6
   correlational studies, 5
   empirical, 3, 31
   evolving nature of, 7–10
   experimental studies, 3–4
   invented spelling supported by, 82, 87
   meta-analyses (*See* meta-analyses)
research findings, 11, 12
   on articulatory pictures and mouth moves, 50–52
   on comprehension strategies, 125–126, 130–131
   on decodable texts, 57–59
   on executive function and cognitive flexibility, 156–157
   on expository text structures, 137–139
   on handwriting instruction, 91–92
   on high-frequency words, 73–75
   on invented spelling, 82–84
   on language comprehension interventions, 162–163
   on letter introduction, 19–20
   on number of times decoding words to learn them, 65–66
   on oral repeated reading, 100–102
   on phonemic/phonological awareness, 41–44
   on print concepts, 31–34
   on reader-text matching, 171–172
   on reading with expression/prosody, 107–108
   on sentence comprehension and syntactic awareness, 146–147
   on teaching letter names and sounds, 25–26
   on text structure, 137–139
   on vocabulary instruction and knowledge, 114–116
research studies, 11, 12
   analyzing and comparing, 6
   on articulatory pictures and mouth moves, 50
   on comprehension strategies, 125, 130
   on decodable texts, 56
   on executive function and cognitive flexibility, 155
   on expository text structures, 137
   on handwriting instruction, 90
   on high-frequency words, 73
   on invented spelling, 82
   on letter names and letter sounds, 25
   on number of letters to introduce per week, 18
   on number of times decoding words to learn them, 65
   on oral language development, 162
   on oral repeated reading, 100
   on phonological awareness, 41
   on print concepts, 30
   on prosody/reading with expression, 106
   on reader-text matching, 170–171
   on sentence comprehension and syntactic awareness, 146
   on text structure, 137
   on vocabulary knowledge/instruction, 114
resources, 13
   on articulatory instruction, 54
   on comprehension strategies, 128, 133
   on decodable texts, 62
   on executive function and cognitive flexibility, 159
   on expository text structures, 142–143
   on handwriting instruction, 95
   on high-frequency words, 79
   on invented spelling, 87
   on number of exposures to decode a word, 70
   on oral language development, 166–167
   on phonemic/phonological awareness, 47
   on phonological awareness, 47
   on print concepts, 38
   on prosody/oral reading expression, 110–111
   on reader-text matching, 175
   on repeated reading and wide reading, 104
   on sentence comprehension, 151–152
   on teaching letter names/sounds, 28
   on text structure, 142–143
   on vocabulary knowledge/instruction, 120
responsive talk, 163, 164
rhymes/rhyme awareness, 42, 43, 44–45, 47
riddles, wordplay, 158

S

Santat, Dan, 119
Scarborough's Reading Rope, 145, 162
Scarborough's Rope model of reading, 8–9
Science of Reading (SoR)
   concerns about, 1
   executive function instruction research and, 157
   explained, 2
   handwriting and, 93
   invented spelling and, 81, 82
   narrow interpretations of, 2
   oral language development and, 161
   sentence comprehension and, 150
   Simple View of Reading and, 8
scientific experiments. *See* experimental studies
Sedita, Joan, 148
segmentation, phonemic, 43, 45–46, 51, 52
self-teaching, 63, 64, 66, 67, 68
sentence combining and reduction, 148–149, 150

sentence comprehension, 145–152
sentences
    practicing high-frequency words in, 79
    understanding between letters, words and, 34
sequential text structure, 135, 136, 139–140
set for variability, 72
shared reading, 33, 34–36
sight recognition, 8, 74
sight words, 19, 71, 72, 74–75. *See also* high-frequency words
signal words, 135, 136, 138, 139, 140, 141
Simple View of Reading, 8, 90, 105, 161
Simple View of Writing, 90
single-syllable words, 57
small-group discussions, for basal programs, 127
small-group instruction, 6
    fluency practice in, 108, 116
    language comprehension interventions and, 162
    for oral language development, 165
    phonemic awareness instruction in, 41, 44
smoothness, on Multidimensional Fluency Scale, 109
sound wall pictures (articulatory pictures), 49, 50
SPAAR (Semantic and Phonological Ability to Adjust Recoding), 72
spectograms, 107
spelling(s)
    handwriting instruction and, 93
    influence on learning less-regular words, 73
    invented, 81–87
    learning words and, 66
    phonemic awareness and, 41–42
spiraling, text-structure instruction and, 141
Strategies at Work, 124
struggling readers. *See also* at-risk students; reading difficulties, students with
    reader-text matching and, 173–174
    repeated oral reading and, 100
    sensitive to text difficulty, 172
SWELL (Strategy Instruction on the Web for English Learners) program, 139

syntactic awareness/complexity, 145–152

T

TALK strategy, 165
teacher talk
    categories of, 163
    self-assessment of, 164–165
    that promote students' oral language, 164
temporary spelling, 82
texts
    matching students and reading level to, 169–175
    prosody and difficulty of, 107, 108–110
    reading the same *versus* multiple, 99–104
    for reading with expression/prosody, 109
text structures, 135–143
time lines, 141
TOWRE assessment, 101
Transactional Strategies Instruction (TSI), 124, 125–126, 139
translational graphics, 13
TSI instruction, 124, 125–126, 139
two-syllable words, 57
typically developing (TD) readers, 73

V

verbal reasoning, 9, 162
visual memorization, 75, 76
visual symbols, 68–69
vocabulary and vocabulary knowledge/instruction
    in Active View of Reading, 10
    correlational studies and, 5
    important role of knowledge of, 113
    influence on learning less-regular words, 73
    language comprehension and, 162
    pre-teaching, 114
    sample weekly routine for, 121–122
    in Scarborough's Rope model, 9
    teacher talk and, 163
voice-to-print match, 32, 33
Vygotsky, Lev, 35

W

"What's Hot in Literacy" survey, 105
whole-group instruction/reading, 6
    handwriting instruction, 93
    language comprehension interventions and, 162
    teaching print concept during shared, 34–36, 37
Wide Fluency-Oriented Reading Instruction (Wide-FORI), 104
wide reading (continuous reading), 99, 100–102, 103, 104
word decodability. *See* decodability
word-learning strategies, 113
    impact on vocabulary knowledge, 115
    for vocabulary instruction, 117–118
word parts, vocabulary and building knowledge of, 117
wordplay riddles, 158
word recognition
    in Active View of Reading, 9
    impact of wide reading and repeated reading on, 101–102
    prosody and, 106, 108
    Scarborough's Rope model on, 8
    text difficulty and, 171
    wide reading and repeated reading impacting, 102
words
    in context *vs.* in isolation, 66
    decoding support for unknown, 174
    influence of regularity of, 73
    irregular/less-regular, 57, 72, 73, 74, 75
    number of times decoding in order to learn, 63–70
    pointing to, 36–37
    and print referencing, 35
    pseudowords, 64
    reader-text matching and complexity of, 174
    repetition of decoding, to map into memory, 61–70
    research findings on children's understanding of, 31–32
    understanding between letters, sentences and, 34
working memory, 90, 129, 154, 156
writing
    four elements of creating a written message, 90
    grammar instruction and, 145–149
    text-structure instruction and, 138, 140, 142
written expression, handwriting instruction improving, 91

Acknowledgments

Thanks to the doctoral students who challenged me with sharp and insightful observations as we read research together.
—*Heidi Anne Mesmer*

Thanks to all the teachers we have worked with over the years. Your questions and passion for growing readers inspire and motivate us.
—*Katie Hilden*

Many thanks to the TCM team, especially Tom Rademacher, who enthusiastically and patiently supported this important book. Many thanks also to Danny Miller, whose positivity and kindness shines through digitally, and to Courtenay Fletcher, Colleen Pidel, and Patricia Corpuz.
—*Heidi Anne and Katie*

About the Authors

Heidi Anne E. Mesmer, Ph.D., is a professor of literacy in the School of Education at Virginia Tech. She has studied beginning reading materials, text difficulty, and struggling readers since 1999. Her research has appeared in *Reading Research Quarterly, The Educational Researcher, Elementary School Journal,* and *Early Childhood Research Quarterly*. She has written and directed multiple grants aimed at improving reading instruction in K–5 classrooms. Dr. Mesmer is regularly called upon by states and professional organizations to deliver lectures in her area of expertise. She is the author of several books.

Katie Hilden, Ph.D., is a professor of literacy in the School of Teacher Education and Leadership at Radford University, where she serves as coordinator of the literacy education graduate program. Her research interests include reading comprehension and cycles of professional learning in literacy. Her work regularly includes partnering with school districts to engage K–8 teachers and reading specialists in cycles of professional learning. In addition to co-authoring multiple book chapters, she has published in *Reading in Virginia* and *Reading and Writing Quarterly*.